ARCHITECTS ON ARCHITECTS

ARCHITECTS ON ARCHITECTS

Susan Gray, Editor

Foreword by Paul Goldberger

McGraw-Hill
*New York • Chicago • San Francisco • Lisbon • London
Madrid • Mexico City • Milan • New Delhi
San Juan • Seoul • Singapore • Sydney • Toronto*

McGraw-Hill

A Division of The ***McGraw-Hill*** *Companies*

1 2 3 4 5 6 7 8 9 0 DOC/DOC 0 7 6 5 4 3 2 1

ISBN 0-07-137583-X

The sponsoring editor for this book was Wendy Lochner and the production supervisor was Sherri Souffrance. It was set in Kennerley by Potter Publishing Studio.

Printed and bound by R. R. Donnelley & Sons Company.

McGraw-Hill books are available at special quantity discounts to use as premiums and sales promotions, or for use in corporate training programs. For more information, please write to the Director of Special Sales, Professional Publishing, McGraw-Hill, Two Penn Plaza, New York, NY 10121-2298. Or contact your local bookstore.

This book is printed on acid-free paper.

Library of Congress Cataloging-in-Publication Data

Gray, Susan.

Architects on architects / Susan Gray.

p. cm.

Includes index.

ISBN 0-07-137583-X

1. Architecture. I. Title.

NA2560.G74 2001

720'.92'2—dc21 2001034550

PREVIOUS SPREAD: **Ricardo Legorreta's Plaza Reforma Corporate Center, Mexico City, 1993. (Legorreta's essay on José Villagrán starts on page 98.)**

PHOTO ON PREVIOUS SPREAD: LOURDES LEGORRETA

Contents

Foreword by *Paul Goldberger* vii
Acknowledgments x
Introduction xiii

Diana Agrest on Sergei M. Eisenstein 2
Tadao Ando on Le Corbusier 10
Henry N. Cobb on H. H. Richardson 18
Norman Foster on Paul Rudolph 26
Mario Gandelsonas on Mies van der Rohe 32
Michael Graves on Le Corbusier 38
Vittorio Gregotti on Peter Behrens 46
Charles Gwathmey on Louis I. Kahn 54
Hugh Hardy on William Van Alen 62
Arata Isozaki on Le Corbusier 70
Carlos Jimenez on Luis Barragan 82
Sumet Jumsai on Le Corbusier 90
Ricardo Legorreta on José Villagrán 98
William S. W. Lim on Le Corbusier 106

Richard Meier on Frank Lloyd Wright 114
William Pedersen on Rockefeller Center 122
Cesar Pelli on Eero Saarinen 128
James Stewart Polshek on Louis I. Kahn 138
Antoine Predock on the Alhambra 146
Raj Rewal on the Unknown Architect of Fatehpur Sikri 154
Richard Rogers on the Maison de Verre 164
Der Scutt on Paul Rudolph 174
Robert A. M. Stern on Paul Rudolph 182
Hans Busso von Busse on Paul Rudolph 190

Selected Works and References 200
About the Editor 217

Foreword

by Paul Goldberger

ABOUT ARCHITECTS, like politicians, it's often best to put your stock in what they do, not in what they say. Few architects are the best commentators on their own work, and even the writings of those architects who produced great quantities of well-remembered words, like Frank Lloyd Wright or Le Corbusier, rarely offer the clearest insight into their buildings.

But ask an architect to write about someone else's architecture, about some other piece of design that has shaped his or her sensibility, and the result is something different entirely. Gone is the arrogance that so often marks architects' writing about themselves, gone is the defensiveness, the attempt to prove that they have found the answer. When architects of great reknown write about their masters, or about the works that formed them, they take on a humility that is otherwise absent. They become students again, and they remember when they were less formed, less certain about everything. In the way that great students always have, they take joy in communicating the thrill of discovery.

These essays are as exciting for their choices of subject as for the substance of their texts. Who would have guessed that Diana Agrest would have chosen to write about Sergei Eisenstein and the way that film—especially the work of this architect-turned-filmmaker—influenced her own architecture? It is probably no surprise that Cesar Pelli paid homage to Eero Saarinen, his mentor and former employer, but that Robert A. M. Stern would write about Paul Rudolph, the dean of the Yale School of Architecture during his student days and the man who embodied a kind of rigid, inflexible modernism that Stern has spent most of his own career reacting against. Stern is now himself the dean of Yale, but this is more than just a younger man learning what it is like to walk in the shoes of an older one. Norman Foster, Der Scutt, and Hans Busso von Busse have also chosen to write about Rudolph, making him the equal, at least among the architects in this volume, of Le Corbusier.

There is great pleasure to me in that, since I believe that Rudolph, an infuriating, difficult genius, has for too long been remembered for his difficulty more than for his genius. His prominence in this volume is surely a sign of the resurgence of his reputation. There is a handful of other surprises here: Antoine Predock's choice of writing on the Alhambra and Raj Rewal's decision to write about Fatehpur Sikri, the capital of the Moghol Empire during the sixteenth century. Henry N. Cobb chose Henry Hobson Richardson, suggesting that his relationship to the great nineteenth-century architect, put to a severe test when Cobb placed the exquisite glass slab of the John Hancock Tower right beside Richardson's voluptuous Trinity Church in Boston in the mid-1970s, is still playing itself out. I suspect that there are similar issues behind Hugh Hardy's choice of William Van Alen and the Chrysler Building and William Pedersen's decision to write about Rockefeller Center—in both cases, New York architects have chosen something that influenced them in their formative years, and which they, symbolically if not literally, continue to go up against every day. Hardy aspires to outdo the Chrysler Building as he tries to jazz up New York, while Pedersen, a prolific designer of corporate skyscrapers, knows that Rockefeller Center remains the great model of the twentieth century.

There might also be something unexpected in Richard Meier's decision to write about Fallingwater, Frank Lloyd Wright's great house for the Kauffmann family in western Pennsylvania, rather than about Le Corbusier, with whom his work is much more often compared. Meier acknowledges this and uses it to offer a striking degree of insight into his own architecture. ("I do not think about Wright, nor do I think about his buildings, when I am doing my own work," Meier writes. "Wright of course did it one way and I do it another. In my opinion, Wright was wrong in some of the things that he said. But I find that interesting. You can learn as much from the oppositions as you can from the strengths.")

At the end of the day it's the essay itself, of course, and not whether its subject matter comes as a surprise, that matters. As I read and reread these essays I realized that they divide themselves in another way from the expected versus the unexpected choice of subject. Some of the essays are primarily about the writer, the person inspired, while others are primarily about the architect or the thing that has been inspirational. It's a fine line, of course, since it isn't possible to acknowledge a great influence on your work without talking a bit about yourself and what you have done. But a few of these chapters have sections that remind me of those eulogies in which well-meaning people attempt to pay respect by talking only about themselves and how well they knew the departed.

A happy exception is Arata Isozaki's remarkable homage to Le Corbusier, "Eros of the Sea," that can stand on its own as an important essay on the great architect. Isozaki is present in this essay only as the writer; he never mentions a single one of his own buildings or discusses his own work explicitly, but it is clear from every sentence how powerful Le Corbusier's influence on Isozaki's architecture was. Isozaki writes of himself standing in Le Corbusier's great monastery of la Tourette, in France, and realizing that the architect had an almost erotic connection to the sea, and of how it affected his architecture. "For Le Corbusier, the sea was the substance of motive force that provoked all of this imagination by permeating every detail of his body," Isozaki writes. "The space of the monastery contains a sheer darkness like the deepest reaches of the sea, totally indescribable and seductive, as if it, too, would irresistibly draw us into it."

Richard Rogers's essay on Pierre Chareau and the Maison de Verre in Paris is more autobiographical, but equally moving. He tells the story of his first visit to the extraordinary glass house, and how completely he was fascinated by "the magnificent space, the way you move through the space, the innovative use of new materials, and, above all, that amazing soft light that infuses space. It was the light that was the most amazing thing—a magical mixture of direct and diffused light, something that I have never seen before. . . . The glowing light magically leads one towards an open stairway and then on and up to the salon. The house feels very much alive with its neverending spirals and labyrinths of perforated metal screens, steel, and glass. It glows with humanness."

That, of course, is what the best of these essays do for architecture itself. They bring us into the process not just of making buildings but of making a sensibility, of making feelings and ways of seeing. All of them, from the most self-absorbed to the most selfless, reveal their writers as people who think and learn, and whose ideas do not spring full-blown from their heads, but which have been formed, slowly, over time. These essays all teach us something about great architecture, but more important, every one of them says something about the nature of influence, and how sometimes it can be a matter of a single work, sometimes an entire career, and sometimes just an attitude and a way of looking that alters another person's life. In every one of these essays we see how an encounter with architecture has changed the direction of a life, and that alone makes this book "glow with humanness."

Acknowledgments

With love and appreciation to:
Charles Evans, Joanne Wang (my agent), Bernard Bauchet, Nannette and Peter Bloch, Joan Brunskill, Carter Horsley, Michael Klingher, Kevin Kushel/OvoWorks, Bill McCuddy, Richard Meier, Chappy Morris, Cable Neuhaus, Brian Palmer, Melanie and James Schaeffer, Joyce Stoner, Yuko Royer, Jamie Wyeth.

I am very fortunate to be able to say thank you to the USG Corporation:

Brian Golden,
Director of Marketing, Architectural Segments;
Robert Grupe,
Director, Architectural and Technical Solutions;
Rik Master,
Manager, Architectural Systems.

Gratitudes to my mother, Vera Paulsen; Linda Munson, Robert Branigan, Beverly Adler and David Brown, Shauna and Jeff Binswanger, Sue and Frank Binswanger, Diane de la Begassiere, Helen Brunskill, Terry D'Ignazio, Erica and Ray Disch, Robert Evans, Fondation Le Corbusier (Madame Evelyne Trehin), Larry Fuerisch, Gabriela Grisi, Jill Goularte, the Gray family, Robin and Marty Gubernick, Caroline Hancock, Beth Harrison, Tami Hausman, Instituto Nacional de Belles Artes/Sara Topelson, Gary Jaffee, Lynn and Richard King, Wilson and Trish King, Ray Krell, Lourdes Legorreta, Carol Leroy, Caren Litherland, Celeste Long, Tom Mellins, Colin Munro, Nikon (Sam Garcia), Gheri Sackler, Elke Wallat-Schopke, Charles Sullivan (Sullivan and Heard), Tim Thayer, Robert Torday, Marilyn and Martin Tully, Ernst Wagner (Paul Rudolph Foundation), Frolic Weymouth, Margi Whitmer, Nicholas Wyeth.

McGraw Hill: Scott Grillo, Dagmar Burdette, Eileen Lewin, Wendy Lochner, Thomas Kowalczyk, Jennifer Nier, Beth Schacht, Margaret Webster-Shapiro, Sherri Souffrance, Stephen Smith, Kieran Walsh.

Potter Publishing Studio: Jeff Potter, Soren Johnson, Renée Southwick, Benjamin Shippee, Hilly van Loon.

Michael Abramson, David Adler and Charlotte Parker, Advance Media Design, Charles E. Alsop, American Book Jam (Ayumi Maki), American Museum of Natural History (Mark Katzman), Americas Society (Victoria Sanchez), Yoshiko Amiya, Lori Andiman (Arthur Pine Associates), Yumiko Ando, Linda Archad, Archipress (Jacqueline Salmon), Architectural Institute of Japan (Maki Yasumori), Archivision (Scott Gilchrist), Art 4d, Artists Rights Society (Janet Hicks), Farshid Assassi, Associated Press (Suzanne Lamis), Association des Amis de Maison de Verre (Gregoire Triet, Dominique Vellay), Avery Library (Angela Giral, Jim Epstein, Janet Parks, Dwight Primiano), Jim Balga, Carla Dorea Bartz (Hector Babenco), Bauhaus-Archiv (Sabine Hartmann), Marta Benach, Michel Benjamin, Benson Latin American Collection (Ann Hartness), Boston Public Library (Janice Chadbourne, Aaron Schmidt), Brandywine River Museum (Halsey Spruance), Veronica Brelsford, Bridgeman Art Library (Liz Boyle), B.O. Abbe Bolle-Reddat (Chapelain De Notre-Dame Du Haut), Christy Brown, Brigitte Brozenec, Canadian Center of Architecture (Louise Désy), Sophie Carter, Center for Creative Photography (Leslie Calmes and Diane Nilson), Centre Georges Pompidou (Christine Sorin),Emilia Ceribelli, Eleanor Clark, Fred Clark, David Patrick Columbia (*Quest*), Columbia University (Suzanne Trimel), COPIA (Swan Day), Dean Coon, Jovey Couldrey, Couvent La Tourette (Antoine Lion and Frere J. P. B. Olivier), Sharon Corporan, Maru Crespo, Linda Crowley, Robert Damora, Peter Dixon, Katherine Dunn, Esto (Christine Cordazzo and Erica Stoller), Charles Evans, Jr., Douglas and AJ Fiorella, Bruce Fleming, Gerard Forde, Forum for Contemporary Art (Dana Turkovic), Galerie Michele Chomette, David Gauld, Dennis Gilbert, Gilman Paper Company (Maria Umali), Alvin Goldfarb, Lisa Green, Suzanne Greenberg, Mig Halpine, Regina Harris, Joel Hecker, Paul Hester, Historic New Harmony (Annie Owen and Kathleen Linderman), Barbara and Simon Hirth–Strauss, Houghton Library (Harvard College Library) Ann Anninger, Laura Khudari), John Howey, Melissa Hsu, Kimberly Hu, *Interiors and Sources* (Martina Scanlan), Yasuhiro Ishimoto, Helmut Jacoby, David Jenkins, Mimmo Jodice, Eric Johanson, Teh Joo-Heng, Sebastian Kaempf, Tan Kah-Heng, A. Kamprasert, Barbara Karant, Adrienne Kennedy, Ann Kirschner, Deborah Kirschner, Sabu Kohso and Judy Geib, K. R. Krishnan/K. Radhakrishnan, Elizabeth Kubany, Ann Lally, Benjamin Lee, Michelle Leong, Lexington Labs (Lucy, Lars, Larra), Kevin Lim, Chris Little, Ian Luna, Vicky MacGregor, Madan Mahatta, John Mandel, Mapin Publishers (Bin Shah), Andrea Martiradonna, Shinoa Matos, Mitsuo Matsuoka, Cristiana Mazza, Ministry of Culture Brasilia, Marianne Mitchell, Mrs. Joseph W. Molitor, Linda and Julio Montes, Julia Moran, Michael Moran, Alberto Muciaccia, Jo Murtagh, Museum of Modern Art Library (Jennifer Tobias), National Geographic Society (Marcia Kebbons, Rob Henry), New York Public Library, Sigrid Neubert, New Millennium Experience Center (Jacinta Johnston and Lisa Sawyer), Louis Noelle, Enrique Norten, Shigeo

Ogawa, Yusuke Okabayashi, Heidi Parker, Kenneth Pearlman, Robert Polidori, Steve Prezant, Profile, Max Protech Gallery, Jeanette Raby, Robert Reck, Resnicow Schroeder (Sascha Freudenheim and Anja Wodsak), Rockefeller Center (Nora Keane and Jim Reed), Ruder Finn (Jennifer Essen and Dana Larson), Lew Rudin (Lee Ann Kennedy), Vanessa Ruff, Saint Paul's School (Mike Barwell), Sarasota County Historical Resources Unit (Ann Shank), Susan Schmidt (Association of Teachers of Japanese), Erma Schmidt-Starz (Photo Art), Mesaaki Sekiya, SJA+3D, Smithsonian Institution (Caroline Weaver), Sotheby's (Katherine Holt), Spencer Theater for the Performing Arts (Brad Cooper), Mary Stone, William P. Stoneman, John Stevenson Gallery, Susan Strauss, Tim Street-Porter, Peter Strongwater, Syracuse University Library (Carolyn Davis, Ed Galvin, and Lucy Sudlow), Brian Brace Taylor, Jason Tax, Emilia Terragani, Thockmorton Gallery (Marlin Barth), Marcia Tiede, Thomas Watson Library (The Metropolitan Museum of Art), Robert Torday, Tourist Office of Spain (Esther Gomez, Alvaro Renedo, and Pilar Vico), Tulane University of Louisiana (Professor Hugh Lester), The University of Arizona/Center for Creative Photography (Leslie Calmes and Marcia Tiede), The University of Pennsylvania (Bill Whitaker), Victor Varganov (St. Petersburg at Your Fingertips), Ron Wallen (Siesta Holidays/Sarasota, Florida), Paul Warchol, Jens Weber, Wellesley College Archives (Jean N. Berry), Western Pennsylvania Conservancy (Clinton Piper), Dae Wha-Kang, Wittliff Gallery/Robert Tejada, Rachel Wohler, World Wide Photos (Bill Fitzgerald), Roy Wright, Yale University Library Manuscript and Archives (Bernice Parent, Diane Kaplan, Danelle Moon, Suzanne Warner and Judy Schiff),Yerba Buena Art Center (Kena Frank), Hirokazu Yokose, Nigel Young.

Introduction

Lost, is it, buried? One more missing piece?
But nothing's lost. Or else: all is translation
And every bit of us is lost in it. . . [1]

—James Merrill

ARCHITECTS ON *ARCHITECTS* is a collection of essays about the different influences recalled by leading architects of today's world, who in return have influenced our lives. When asked how they arrive at their ideas, architects, like artists, confess that they really do not know. Some, however, vividly remember "the moment."

Arata Isozaki talks of a sudden moment when "I came across a scene in which a brightly colored altar was illuminated by bundles of light shining through the cylindrical windows, *canon de lumière*, I was more than surprised; I was intoxicated by ecstasy . . . . [t]he Convent Sainte-Marie de la Tourette is the place where I realized that a space could cause a sensation akin to sexual intercourse. . . "

It was also "the moment" for Tadao Ando when he first saw the Chapelle Nôtre Dame du Haut, "Because of the overwhelming spatial experience, which penetrated deep into my soul, I had to escape after staying less than one hour. I was awestruck by a light unprecedented in my life."

Many architects are reluctant to credit influences. Yet all of the contributors in *Architects on Architects* have taken the past and have made it their own. To them, "influence" is not a dirty word. They have found that the search for self-realization goes *beyond* the self. To them, influence is part of the ongoing process.

Hence, to write about influences is a slippery thing, for it depends upon memory, and memory has a mind of its own. Prejudices, projections, nostalgia are selective translations of the past. It is in this labyrinth of time that many become lost. Yet these influential architects, master weavers of contradictions, continue in all time.

"I believe in the choice of an ideal maestro," writes Vittorio Gregotti, "of a reference to whom to go with the soul, as well as with the mind, at the moment of the constitution of the project. A maestro is all the more important, however, the more we become aware of what differentiates us from him, looking at him as a point of reference to measure the detachment, the distance that divides us as much as the line that connects us."

Carlos Jimenez writes, "[Barragan's] work revealed the power of its emotive manifesto: a poetic interlude between the inevitability of space and the wonder of nature. . . . Barragan's work ultimately reminds me of the great Russian filmmaker Andrei Tarkovsky's reflections on the creative act: 'Perhaps the meaning of all human activity lies in artistic consciousness, in the pointless and selfless creative act? Perhaps our capacity to create is evidence that we ourselves were created in the image and likeness of God?' "

A journey to the beginning or "a return, so to say, to the old (negation of the negation)." [2]

But, you ask, "Aren't all memories lies?"

Does it matter? What else do we have? How else can we discover the creative process by which an artist's work develops?

But remember this: We don't own our memories—they own us.

"Your memory is a monster; you forget—it doesn't." John Irving wrote in *A Prayer for Owen Meany*. "It simply files things away. It keeps things from you—and summons them to your recall with a will all its own. You think you have a memory, but it has you."

What we see influences how we feel about things in life. And architecture is the reflection of our collective civilization.

We are not only the architects of our memories and builders of our dreams but also of our homes and of our cities, and for this we have a responsibility. Hence, the question is not what has been built but what should be built.

Architecture can alter the identity of a city or even a whole nation. Architecture can outrage us, enlighten us, and even physically arouse us, for buildings have a language filled with gestures, moods, colors, personalities, and eccentricities. Yet to the untrained eye, buildings do not speak. They are made mute only by ignorance—by our unwillingness to even consider a dialogue.

To have great architecture, we need to have a great audience.

"It was also a period when my clients tended to be 'building committees' often dominated by finance members," writes Raj Rewal. "If driven to the wall, I could always appeal to the poetic sensibilities of one or two members to achieve desired architectural results . . . perhaps an illiterate monarch [Akbar, who oversaw the design of Fatehpur Sikri] is not different from an anonymous organization that works through committees [. . . yet] historically it is well established that Akbar . . . took risks and encouraged creativity."

Does architecture have to be feverishly entertaining to be recognized?

How much architecture do we really see? Do buildings just appear? Do buildings just disappear? What is it that we expect from our architecture? How much are we, the users, responsible for?

"I was deeply influenced by his [Eero Saarinen's] example," recalls Cesar Pelli. ". . . Architecture is a public art, and its practice presupposes responsibilities to the place and purpose of buildings, to users, clients and society, and to ourselves and our ideals. The hardest and most necessary thoughts in architecture address the difficult interaction between our responsibilities and our artistic goals."

All architecture has presence. And its presence is an affirmation, not a negation, of us—of our lives, our history, and our civilization.

Remember everything, everything is architecture. An ongoing process, a record of time.

"La theorie c'est bonne, mais ca n'empeche pas d'exister." [3]

1 James Merrill; excerpt from "Lost in Translation," in *Divine Comedies* (New York: Atheneum,1976).

2 Vladimir Ilyich Lenin, *Filosofskiye tetradi.* (Moscow: Ogiz, 1947) 192–193.

3 "Theory is good, but it doesn't prevent things from existing."—Charcot

ARCHITECTS ON ARCHITECTS

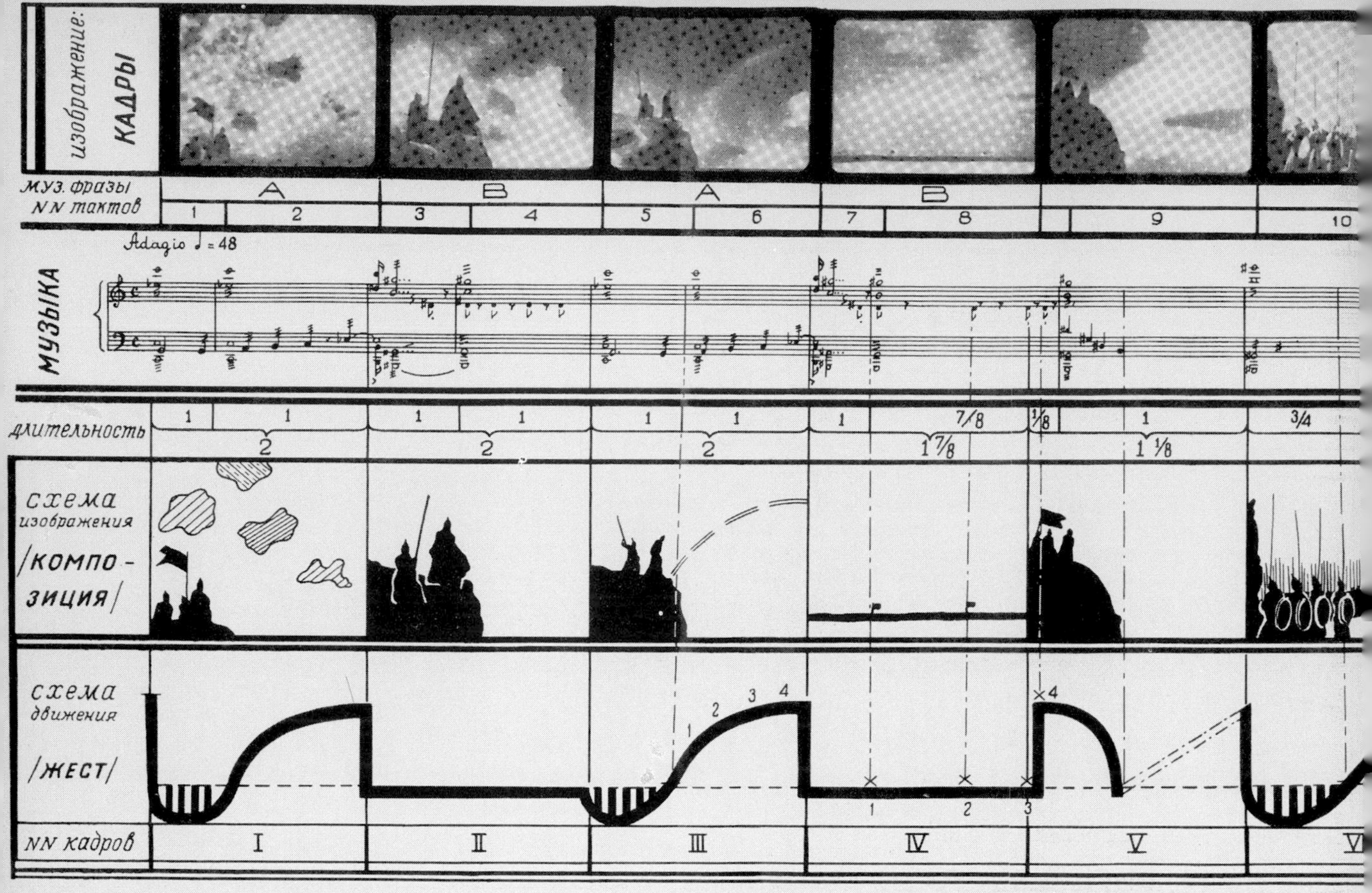

Audiovisual articulation in a sequence from Eisenstein's film *Alexander Nevsky*, 1938.

Diana Agrest *on* Sergei M. Eisenstein

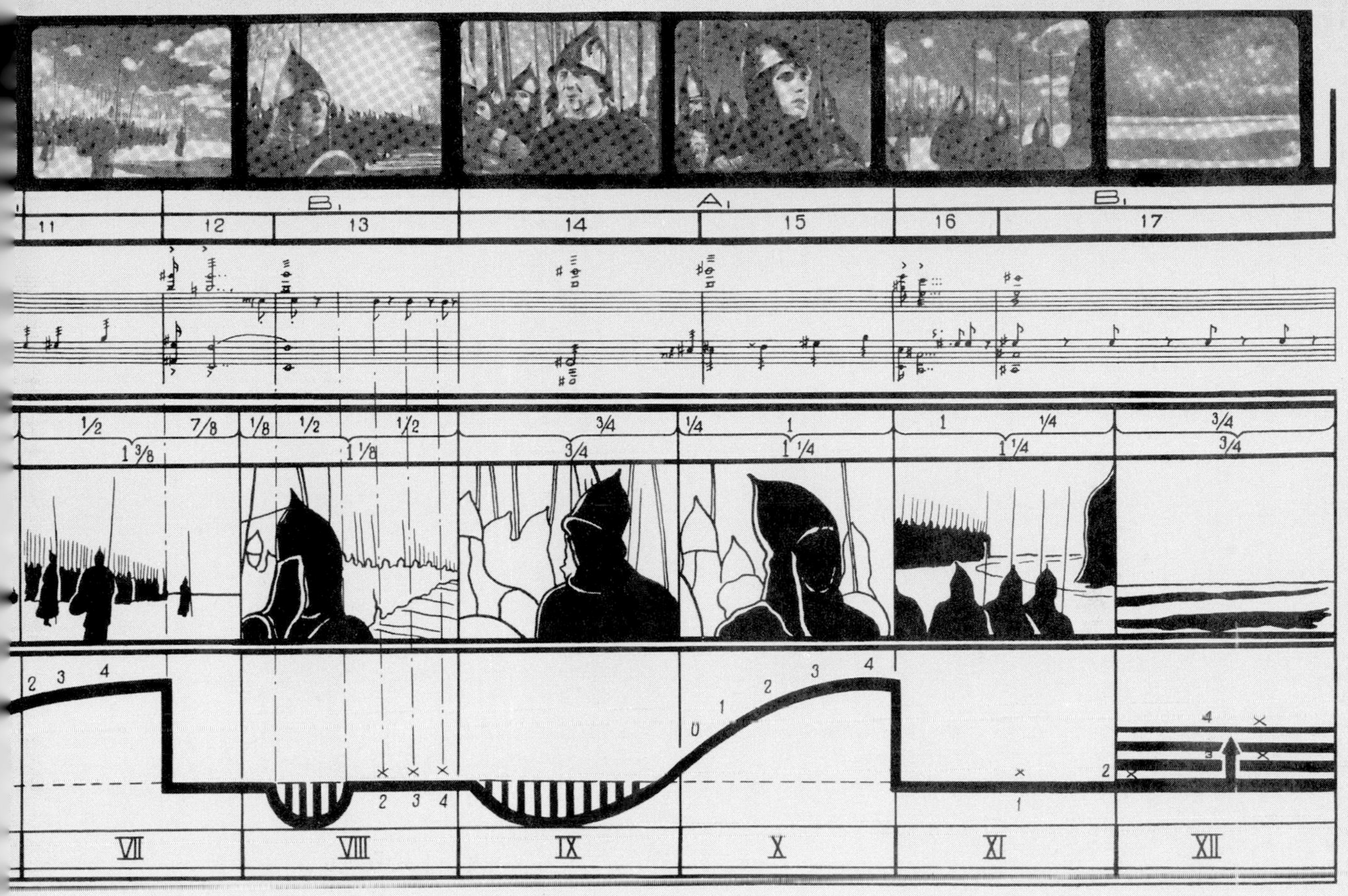

SERGEI MIKHAILOVICH EISENSTEIN

SINCE MY SCHOOL DAYS I have been passionately interested in urban design, an interest that led me, in my pursuit to rethink urban architecture, to develop a critical (theoretical) work in relation to my practice.

I remember distinctly one day in Paris after finishing my studies there (at the EPDHE), writing a short text about how I saw the city as the relationship between urban form and culture. The brief essay was called "Urban Shifters" and was an attempt to think how to incorporate the richness and complexity of the city, that as architects, in a reductive operation, we often filter out. But what I remember most vividly about this writing experience is the feeling for some time that I just did not have the conceptual tools to develop my own ideas further.

It is in this context that film appeared to me as the most pertinent field to relate to the city, one that provided a conceptual framework from which to develop the architectural discourse of the city, and ultimately to promote other modes of architectural production.

Some of the most important concepts that allowed me to pursue those ideas came from film, and not from architecture or urbanism. It was not simply as a discipline that film became paradigmatic of how to think about the city (urban form) but more specifically, Sergei M. Eisenstein (educated as an architect and the son of an architect as well), who provided for me the most enlightened view of how meaning and culture worked in filmmaking, both in theory and in practice. His work, both his extraordinary films and his inspiring writings, was tremendously influential to me. His theory of montage, in which he analyzed how a narrative is developed through the sequential organization of form and image, was of great importance for me in thinking about and producing architecture.

Eisenstein saw filmmaking as various languages working together in a complex set of relationships, like an orchestra score. His graphic synchronization of the various components for the film *Alexandre Nevsky* clearly exemplifies this concept. This approach coincided with the way I was trying to think of the city as the object of architectural practice.

Architecture traditionally has been related to painting and sculpture as the permanent visual testimonies of culture. This has been particularly true since the Renaissance. Together with painting, architecture has been linked to theater in relation to the discovery of perspective and the definition of the theatrical perspectival space. I found that a displacement from painting to film, as the most pertinent visual art to which urban architecture can relate, was necessary.

The city can be examined (considered) as the physical manifestation of the conflicts and contradictions of our society, as the locus of social flows, as the place where the forces of expression, repression, and conflict intersect. Through film, the city can be read in its physicality and its visuality as a literal physical space and as a mediated reality.

(Urban) architecture, (urban) form, can relate to film form as one text to another, in terms of configurations composed of so many fragments of languages organized in time through space. The city, analogous to film, is a continuous open sequence of spaces and objects perceived through time.

Not only did time and movement become clearly pertinent parameters within which to think about the city, but the question of the narrative also appeared as an essential aspect for understanding the city (an aspect that as architects we reduced to a diagrammatic list of functions, when in fact there are in the city a myriad of narratives).

Architectures that include levels of narrative, time, action, etc., that open and erode on the fixed boundaries of each discipline as institutionally defined, are produced by the city itself. Reading the city through film allows access into the complexity, the expansive force, and sequential organization of fragments in time that characterize the city.

ROBERT E. MATES/© THE SOLOMON R. GUGGENHEIM FOUNDATION

Spiral walkway of Wright's Solomon R. Guggenheim Museum, 1959.

In looking retrospectively as I write these notes, I remember another very influential figure on me while I was a very young student—Frank Lloyd Wright, the Wright of Johnson Wax and more particularly the Guggenheim Museum. The Guggenheim was my first experience of "architectural space." In a way, it makes perfect sense that he would be the most influential architect for me early on. What was fascinating to me was how movement and time were one with the architecture. Paintings were seen as frames in a sequence, and looking backward and forward walking along the ramp, one has the feeling of "parallel montage" or even of "racconto." The space unfolded like a filmstrip. It was also the way the various volumes were articulated, superimposed, and juxtaposed, while maintaining their identity in a way that also relates to montage in the sense developed by Eisenstein.

The filmic movement of people throughout the building was such an integral part of this space that to see it just as a monument was missing the essential point of this truly urban architecture. Film became one of the most important referents to me. Just as painting had been historically the most important referent for architecture, I was convinced that film was the referent now that the city had become the most extraordinary architectural production of our time, albeit without an architect.

Eisenstein's theory of the shot, and its decomposition and recomposition through montage and its sequential organization, could provide the architect or the filmmaker with the eye of the camera to read the city. I saw the architect as a film director assembling different materials that in the end made a complex whole.

In the urban projects in particular I have developed two aspects in relation to a filmic reading of the city. One is the "mise-en-sequence" and the other is the production of place—public place—where in fact the complexity of urban culture and form is produced and manifested. Public places relate to each other sequentially, providing the scene for narratives and sometimes the spectacular to occur.

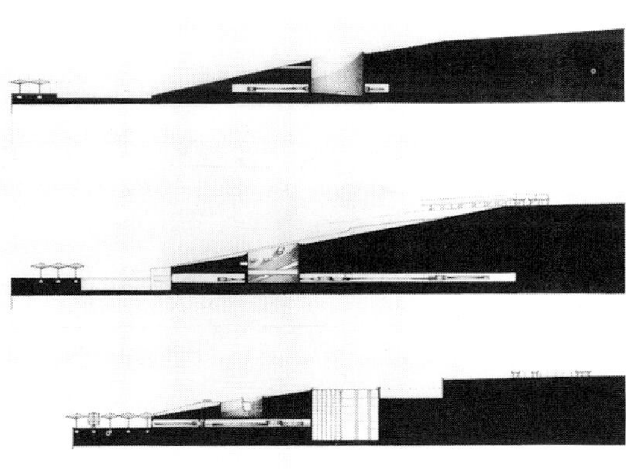

DIANA AGREST

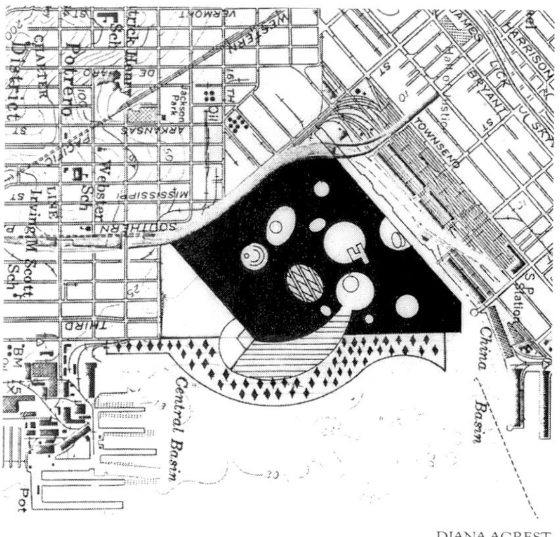

DIANA AGREST

Agrest's China Basin, San Francisco, California, 1989–91.

ABOVE: **Three sections through (*top to bottom*): curvilinear movement system, Olympic Training Center, and Marketplace.** TOP RIGHT: **Plan showing carpet green with curvilinear public spaces.** RIGHT: **The Machine in the Garden—plan showing carpet of green with curvilinear public spaces.**

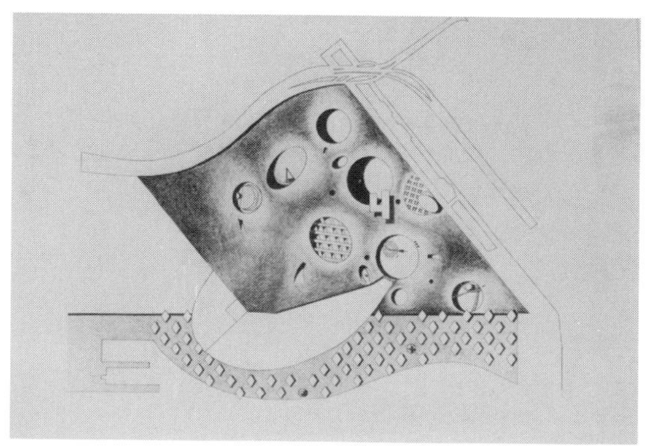

DIANA AGREST

PAUL WARCHOL PHOTOGRAPHY

In China Basin, a project that I have titled "The Machine in the Garden," these concepts have taken precedent over the buildings that have now disappeared, exposing nature as a subject essential to urban discourse, a subject repressed since World War II. The entire complex is a continuous flow from public place to public place along curvilinear movement systems through narratives, which are promoted by the particular activities taking place there and the indetermined and fluctuating boundaries between them under a blanket of green.

We no longer go from the small scale of the house to the large scale of the city. The city determines architecture; the city is the unconscious of architecture.

In the house on Sagpond, consisting of an assemblage of various objects rather than one single building, there is a movement that is created by the superimposition of two geometries: that of the bar—the vaulted volume—and that of the towers and bridges. The wedge left between the two generates

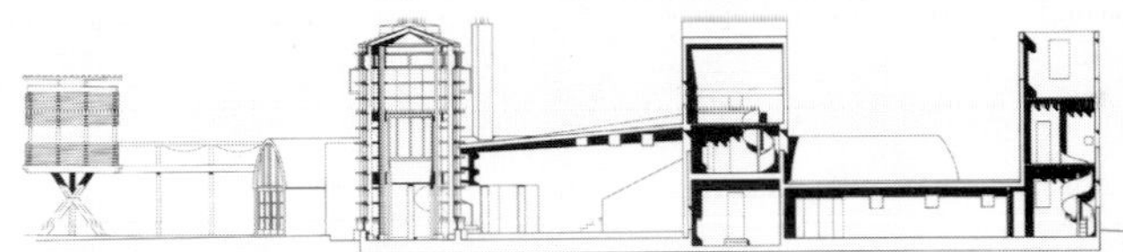

AGREST & GANDELSONAS ARCHITECTS

TOP: **View from the south, house on Sagpond, Sagaponack, New York, 1989–90.** ABOVE: **Longitudinal section, house on Sagpond.**

a movement and creates a different mode of articulation between the towers and the bar. There is an abstract formal structure while at the same time a figurative quality, two terms that had previously been mutually exclusive in modern architecture.

The towers carry a narrative power, which changes just as in montage, as explained very clearly and potently by Eisenstein in his texts on montage and exemplified in his film *October*. Each scene in a montage acquires a different meaning, depending on its placement in a sequence in relation to other scenes.

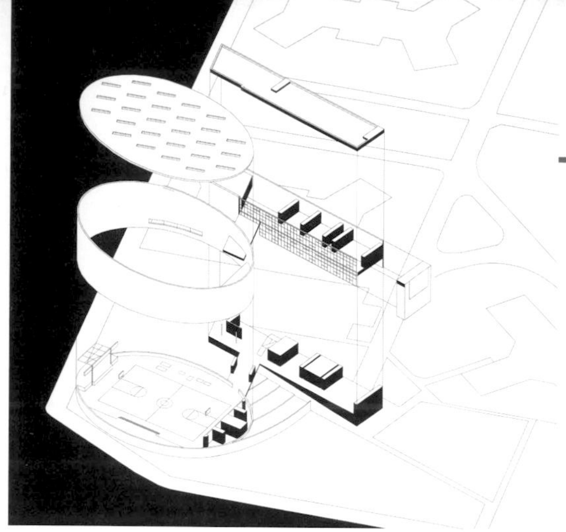

AGREST & GANDELSONAS ARCHITECTS

Diagram of Melrose Community Center, Bronx South, New York, 1995–2000 .

In Sagpond, the towers can be read very differently, depending on what other elements of the house they are perceived with. Thus the "lighthouse" tower can be seen in a time sequence, with the house tower prototype on the waterfront relating to the horizontal band of windows framing the reflections of the very horizontal landscape; not only is it literally the support for the house, but also figuratively, by reflection running under and engaging the towers.

This same tower creates a very different effect as it relates to the southern end of the bar and the cylindrical glass tower. We could do the same operation with each one of the towers, which are almost like ready-made fragments montage in such a way that they generate different possible modes of perception in different time sequences. In walking around the house, it unfolds (narratives) in time through space without a beginning or an end, a planned chance.

In the Melrose Community Center project, both Eisenstein and Wright have been unconsciously present—reinforcing each other—the separate parts of the building preserving their identity while they establish a playful relationship with each other. Movement and sequence are emphasized by the elliptical volume of the gym turning the corner. The transparent "bar" is organized as active frames within transparent activity rooms painted in different colors. This building also presents juxtaposition and contrast between the heritage of modernist urbanism (from

View of the Melrose Community Center from the entry at 156th Street.

where I started) represented in the housing project buildings and the modern architecture of the building.

I could continue to read the work retrospectively and find this influence reappear in various degrees of unconscious interpretation and transformation, as in the more recent Shanghai urban project, where the windows become a theme, particularly the windows on a very large urban scale, where Hitchcock's *Rear Window* seems to have taken over.

Interior view of Le Corbusier's Chapelle Ronchamp Nôtre Dame du Haut, France, 1951.

Tadao Ando *on* Le Corbusier

SINCE THE TIME I determined to become an architect, how many times have I visited this church at Ronchamp? In April 1965, soon after the travel ban on the Japanese general public was lifted, I went on a solitary journey to Europe for the first time in my life. I embarked on a ship at Yokohama and took the Trans-Siberian Railway headed for Europe

TADAO ANDO

Exterior view of Le Corbusier's Chapelle Ronchamp.

in order to meet—as a most important purpose of the trip—Le Corbusier himself. There was no way for a twenty-three year old who had just begun to study architecture by himself, outside the academy, to have had enough knowledge to deeply understand Le Corbusier's architecture. Passion, sheer passion, drove me on that reckless journey. In fact I had been encouraged by Le Corbusier's words in *Vers Une Architecture*, stressing that a journey in one's youth has a deep and strong significance throughout a lifetime. At that time, studying architecture was equal to studying the rational Western architecture. I came to believe that going to Europe was my life necessity. Furthermore, as I traced Le Corbusier's work every day from an *Œuvres Completés* I had encountered in a used bookshop (and had been able to purchase only after a struggle) I became totally fascinated by the mysterious power of his work. I absolutely had to ascertain that power in the presence of the work. And I came to want to meet him in person.

It was around the end of September that I arrived in Paris, after having traveled through Scandinavia. The first thing was to see Le Corbusier's architecture. Taking different trains from Paris for two or three hours, I found the church on top of a small hill in Ronchamp. With great anticipation and excitement, I approached the architecture from below, first glimpsing a part of the roof. It seemed that a giant seashell, such as a mollusk or a crab, loomed on the small hill—such a mysterious impression struck me. This sense is especially strong when the chapel is approached from the south.

This Dominican church has been one of the Holy sites for pilgrimages since the twelfth century. Like the Sainte-Marie de la Tourette monastery, it is one of Le Corbusier's last works, and stands opposite the Unité d'Habitation in Marseilles, which is a synthesis and culmination of the geometric order of the right angle. In contrast, this church is totally exceptional among his works, most of which are regulated by clear logic. I was overwhelmed by this architecture celebrating the joy of creation and human freedom. It is easily imaginable that Le Corbusier, who had little chance to work on architecture during and right after World War II, had channeled his creative energy into painting. But then he designed the church in Ronchamp "with tremendous speed," as if harnessing all the energy for architectural creation he had accumulated during the time he had no freedom. On June 1, 1950, the first day he visited the site, he "sought to create an architecture which, as it were, roars from the ridge, in a dialogue with the land." As soon as he stepped onto the site that day, Le Corbusier began drawing horizontal lines in the four directions; the curve of the south side was drawn almost in one breath. After a number of freehand sketches, he "finished the whole design two days after."

Trying to hold my horses, I stepped into the church and positioned myself in the light streaming in from the openings irregularly scattered across the slanted wall. Light of various intensities and colors—red, blue, and yellow—came in from different angles, and drawing sharp contours on the floor, they clashed intensely. Because of the overwhelming spatial experience, which penetrated deep into my soul, I had to escape after staying less than one hour. I was awestruck by a light unprecedented in my life.

Architectural light, with its color, temperature, texture, and depth, has great power to influence the soul. In the kind of space I had empirically known from Japanese traditional houses—such as *shoin-zukuri* (library style) and *sukiya-zukuri* (tea house style)—light reflects from below. Direct sunlight is blocked and filtered by eaves and *shoji* screens, while the reflections on the *engawa* verandah (outside corridor) and garden softly wrap the inhabitants. On the other hand, the light in Ronchamp was so strong as to disorient me, a person accustomed to the light of Japanese houses. It was then that I realized that this was really an "architecture of light."

With respect to the three towers of light, Le Corbusier confessed that his idea was inspired by the space of ruins of the Villa Adriana that he saw on his

SHIGEO OGAWA

Ando's Church of the Light, Sunday School.

famous Le Voyage d'Orient. But where did the image of innumerable holes come from? It is said that the sources of the images of the white stucco walls and loopholes are the houses and mosques he sketched in 1931 in M'zab, about 600 kilometers south of Algiers; and perhaps he was influenced by the spaces of Mikonos. All in all, though, it is impossible to isolate the source of influence, and it seems to me to be meaningless to try. In the history of architecture or the history of architectural light from ancient times to the present, Le Corbusier's energy must have created a singular space of light.

When I visited the church for a second time, I had gained some experience from my own work. With this new insight, I was able to take into consideration elements other than light. I was fascinated by the sculptural form, which betrayed, as it were, the norm of modern architecture. The sensuous, powerful, and vivid plastic art impressed me as the very "architecture of form."

It is commonly said that Le Corbusier pursued the double image of life and machine. But when an artist creates, logic is not the driving force. He creates because he has superior intuition. The power of intuition opens the possibility of instantaneously creating a condensed world with beauty. It might be said that the essences of various spaces Le Corbusier experienced were intermixed, fermented, and embodied to appear as the one and only one that had never existed before.

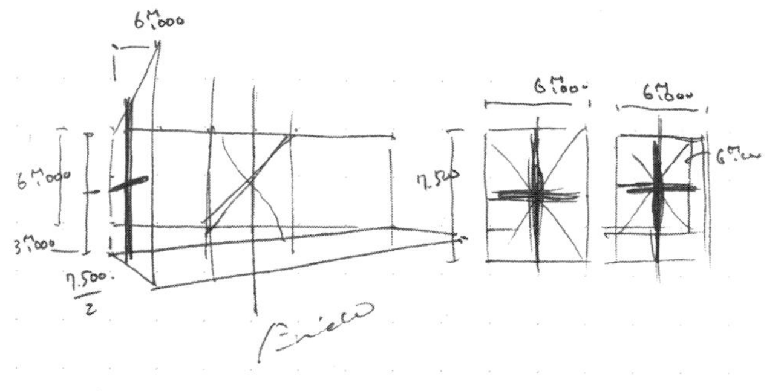

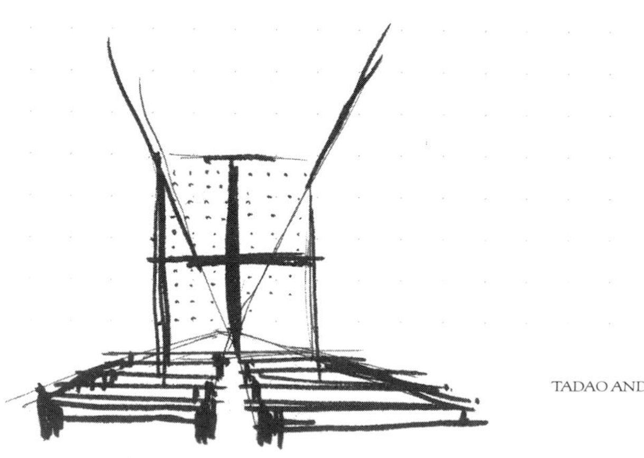

TADAO ANDO

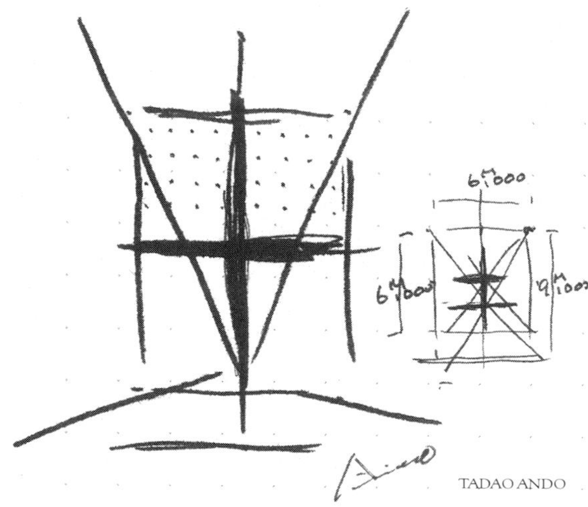

TADAO ANDO

ABOVE AND LEFT: **Drawings of the Church of the Light.** OPPOSITE: **Service in the Church of the Light.**

MITSUO MATSUOKA

TADAO ANDO

Ando's Meditation Space, UNESCO, Paris, France, 1995.

It is said that in the plan of the architecture was an impeccable application of a symbolic system he had developed in his *Le Poeme De l'Angle Droit*, a collection of lithographic works consisting of seven parts and completed between 1947 and 1953. Le Corbusier sought modernist and functionalist expression in architecture; the manifestation of his aesthetics based upon the non-organic model was seen in the publication of the *Modulor*.

On the other hand, in the painting he consistently practiced along with architecture, Le Corbusier sought a symbolic expression based upon alchemy, astrology with a related symbolic language, and Greek mythology; in this, his energetic pulses flapped more and more freely. Here it is impressive that the Mediterranean and sea animals he loved more than anything appear time and again. These elements played major roles, it seems to me, in his later works, including the church in Ronchamp. But it is not that in these works he abandoned the *Modulor*. In fact the plan of the church faithfully follows the square grid of *Modulor*; even the loophole openings, which give us an impression of irregularity, are geometrically ordered according to *Modulor*.

Though this work is functionally simple, conceived as a space of one room, it has an overflowing richness at the same time. In a way, Le Corbusier's way of life was expressed in the architecture; he persisted in being avant-garde throughout his lifetime by oscillating wildly between formal principles and freedom of expression, thereby cultivating the aesthetics for a new age. This architecture stimulates our imagination by evoking innumerable images. While its unique plasticity is ambiguous, it embodies a powerful symbolism. His painting on the front gate, which greets visitors, reminds us of the beach. Also the fact that the word "la mer" is inscribed in the stained glass that overlooks the town from the hill reminds us of his almost instinctive sense of belonging to the sea. As is well known, his life ended in the sea. The sea, the fate of his life. It is the sea that nurtured the life of Le Corbusier as a creator.

It is said that when he constructed the form of Ronchamp, Le Corbusier attempted to carefully respond to the vibration that came from the shape of land, a sort of wave that affects the auditory senses. Le Corbusier later figured acoustics in the domain of form.

When I visited Ronchamp—how many times later I do not remember—a hymn was coincidentally being sung in the chapel. Listening to the voices comfortably echoing around the space, I thought that the architecture was for the song. I felt that the space of architecture became one of sound. The church, which was concretized by the acoustics of the landscape, has an ideal space, literally, for acoustic effects. Thus this time, I thought that this was an "architecture of sound."

Through these experiences I realized that the church of Ronchamp is an architecture that appeals to the five senses. Every time I visit, I discover a new aspect of it affecting a different sense.

With the manifesto of the "Five Principles of Modern Architecture," Le Corbusier persisted in parting from conventional architecture and looking for an architecture of the future world. Distinguished from the simpleminded pursuit of functionalism, his stance was always accompanied by the pursuit of freedom of expression. Le Corbusier, who had oscillated between reason and sensibility and order and freedom, finally, late in his career, designed the Ronchamp church with the full-blown freedom of sensibility.

At the time, the architecture was criticized as signaling a conversion for the architect, who had been dealing with the social and technological problematics of modernist architecture, insisting that "a house is a machine to live in." This architecture, however, played a monumental role in liberating modernism from its hard shell by pointing to the alternative of free expression. As we read in this architecture the manifesto that modern architecture is open to every possibility, we can keep the courage for new challenges.

—*Translated by Sabu Kohso*

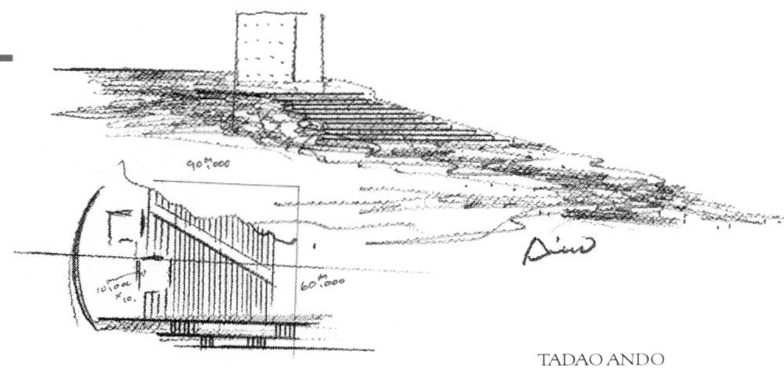

TADAO ANDO

SHIGEO OGAWA

SHIGEO OGAWA

Three views of Ando's Chikatsu-Asuka Historical Museum, Osaka, Japan, 1994. TOP: **Drawing by the architect.** CENTER: **Aerial view.** RIGHT: **Detail of its courtyard.**

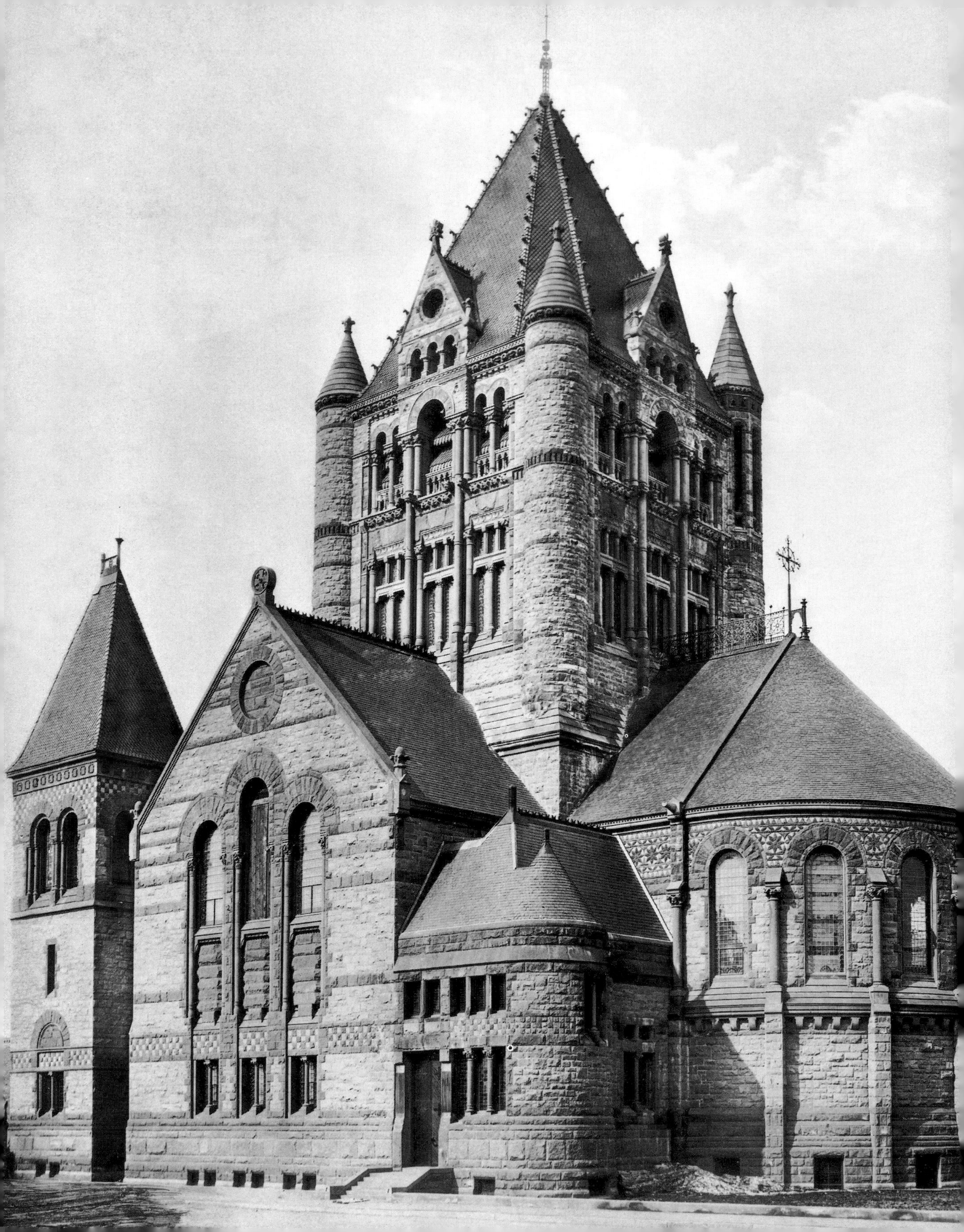

Henry N. Cobb

on

H. H. Richardson

Why Richardson Won

According to legend, H.H. Richardson was fond of declaring that there are just three rules for the successful practice of architecture: Rule one: Get the job! Rule two: Get the job! Rule three: Get the job! Although perhaps apocryphal, this story is surely truthful in suggesting

Richardson's preoccupation with the art of seduction as an indispensable handmaid to the art of architecture—a preoccupation copiously documented in James F. O'Gorman's biography[1] of this exceptionally gifted architect who was also an exceptionally charming man. And nowhere was Richardson's adherence to his three rules more strikingly displayed than in the competition entry that won him the commission to design Trinity Church, a building that would propel him at one stroke to the forefront of his profession.

It has often been noticed by critics and historians—O'Gorman among them—that Richardson's competition design, as represented in a perspective drawing believed to have been the centerpiece of his submission, was compositionally awkward and stylistically confused. As O'Gorman remarks: "The composition as a whole appeared disjointed. In fact critics have often wondered how Richardson won the competition with such a gawky design; certainly his first project was not measurably better than several of those who lost. We do not know," he adds, "specifically what swung the committee in his favor." Indeed we cannot *know*, inasmuch as there are no surviving records of the jury's deliberation. Yet with the compelling evidence of the aforementioned drawing before us, together with parish records documenting the vestry's reasons for acquiring the Copley Square site, we are surely able to *surmise* why Richardson won. He won because he alone among the invited competitors conceived and presented his project as a bold and absolutely unambiguous symbol of the aspirations—both explicit and implicit—that motivated his prospective client's building enterprise.

When, in 1871, the vestrymen of Trinity Church were searching for a site in Boston's fashionable Back Bay, they considered and rejected a number of corner lots similar to those selected by other congregations—including, for example, the Brattle Square (now First Baptist) Church, then under construction, and Richardson's design on Commonwealth Avenue at Clarendon Street. Instead, they chose a relatively remote plot of land projecting into the as yet undeveloped Copley Square. Their motive for choosing this site, explicitly stated in parish records, was that they wanted their new building to be surrounded by streets on all sides, so that as a freestanding edifice it would proclaim Trinity's autonomy and, by implication, its primacy as *the* church in a burgeoning city that then saw itself, not without reason, as "the Athens of America." Richardson surely knew of these motives, and indeed they must have been known to the other invited competitors as well, all five of whom probably had ties of friendship to members of the Trinity parish. But comparison of Richardson's entry with two others that were subsequently published—competent if uninspired exercises in the then popular Gothic Revival style—shows that only he seems to have envisioned intuitively an architecture that would constitute the *built embodiment* of the

OPPOSITE: **Perspective drawing of H. H. Richardson's competition design for Trinity Church, submitted in May 1872.**
PREVIOUS SPREAD: **Trinity Church as it appeared shortly after its completion in 1877.**

DEPARTMENT OF PRINTING AND GRAPHIC ARTS, HOUGHTON LIBRARY, HARVARD COLLEGE LIBRARY

vestry's aspirations. This intuitive capacity, which we would not be wrong to call genius, is vividly evidenced in the very first sketch that Richardson made on the back of the letter inviting him to compete. It depicts a Greek cross, a plan form that is unequivocally autonomous, centralized, self-referential. A design conceived on such a plan—inherently sculptural, demanding to be seen in the round—must have appealed powerfully to minds searching for a work of architecture that would fully validate their choice of site. When we consider Richardson's perspective drawing, gawky and even absurd as it may appear to a critical eye, we cannot fail to marvel that an architect who was not yet entirely the master of his art had nonetheless thoroughly mastered the companion art of seduction—an art practiced here with such consummate skill that even the shape of the drawing, a roundel, emphasizes the strengths of his conception while concealing its weaknesses, and by its cosmic connotations subtly reinforces his claim to be, without question, *the man for the job.*

Although Trinity Church as built is vastly superior to the design represented in Richardson's competition drawing, the strengths and weaknesses of both are remarkably similar in kind—so much so that the "official" Richardson-authorized photograph of the completed building adopted the same viewpoint as that of the competition perspective (though from

COURTESY OF THE BOSTON PUBLIC LIBRARY, PRINT DEPARTMENT. PHOTOGRAPH BY THOMAS E. MARR, 1900

the opposite side), with the clear aim of displaying to best advantage the powerful composition of apse and transept surmounted by a central tower, while concealing the unfinished west front, which the architect never resolved in a form that his client could afford. Unhappily, and ironically, Trinity's disappointing west front, feebly embellished by towers and a porch after Richardson's death, was soon made to appear even more conspicuously wanting by its forced confrontation with the magisterial façade of the Boston Public Library, built to the design of Charles Follen McKim, who as Richardson's assistant had himself drawn the Trinity competition plans.

When, a century later, the Hancock Tower rose

Copley Square as it appeared in 1900, with Trinity Church on the left, the Museum of Fine Arts in the center, and the Boston Public Library on the right.

ROBERT DAMORA

on the block just south of Trinity, it was placed diagonally on its site so as to shape a space that would at last give prominence to the splendid apsidal view of the church, with the larger purpose of restoring this noble if flawed monument to its intended role as the architectural cynosure of Copley Square—inviting the admiration of passersby while allowing them to apprehend, so I like to believe, why Richardson won.

[1] James F. O'Gorman, *Living Architecture: A Biography of H. H. Richardson* (New York: Simon & Schuster Editions, 1997).

ROBERT DAMORA

HENRY N. COBB

LEFT: Conceptual sketch by Henry N. Cobb of the John Hancock Tower in its urban setting. OPPOSITE: Henry N. Cobb's John Hancock Tower and H. H. Richardson's Trinity Church. ABOVE: Trinity Church and the John Hancock Tower, 1977.

Norman Foster

on

Paul Rudolph

IN 1961 PAUL RUDOLPH WAS the main reason that I chose to go to Yale University for the masters course in architecture. As a student, I was familiar with his early works through illustrations in the magazines of the time. His drawings held a particular fascination for me—unlike those of other architects, they were not only graphically seductive but also rigorous in the manner in which they revealed the anatomy and the spatial qualities of his buildings. The architecture itself was to me fresh, radical, and unconventional. I am thinking of those early buildings in Florida with *brise soleil* like white, abstract sculptures, a house with foldout walls and the inverted curve of a cocoon roof—new forms growing out of new materials.

Perspective of the east-west section of Rudolph's Yale Art and Architecture building.

TRUSTEES OF THE PAUL RUDOLPH ESTATE

The scholarship that made my American education possible offered me the choice of Harvard or Yale. It was many years later that I was to read how Paul Rudolph felt deeply indebted to his teacher Walter Gropius when he was a student at Harvard. Rudolph described him as an "educator unsurpassed" and talked about the importance of his education as providing a "point of reference." It is a fitting tribute that so many years later I should feel compelled to write how important Paul Rudolph was to me. I could almost use the same words. I am sure that this is true not only for myself but also for countless individuals who shared the privilege of his direct influence as a teacher and perhaps more indirectly as an architect.

PREVIOUS SPREAD: **Detail of western stairtower, Rudolph's Art and Architecture Building, Yale University, New Haven, Connecticut, 1959–63.**

At Yale, Rudolph was a legend. He would set a short, twenty-four-hour project for the whole school—pitching undergraduates from every year against graduates. In the same spirit, he would summon the masters class a few days before the hand-in of a major design assignment for a snap crit. By then some of us might even be drawing up a final scheme. The ensuing criticism could call into question all of our efforts. The result might mean that the entire project would be discarded, but there would be renewed pressure on everyone to produce a new and better design in the remaining few days. We all knew from his reputation that he would have been able to deliver it himself on an even tighter schedule. It was common knowledge that Rudolph had produced over a weekend the elegant and spatially complex apartment that he occupied a few blocks from the school—not only the design but single-handedly all the production drawings as well!

I remember one Saturday morning when he entertained the masters class away from the studio and in his own personal surroundings. There were some long silences at our meeting, and I realized that in some ways Rudolph was a solitary figure with a side that could be touchingly awkward and shy. By contrast, he was never lost for words in the studio, perhaps because he was fired by his passion for architecture.

My year in the masters class was divided between Paul Rudolph and Serge Chermayeff, who had been recruited from Harvard to take over the running of the school. It was a measure of Rudolph's self-confidence and concern for his students that he would always seek out the strongest leaders in their field—not only to replace himself but also to complement his own presence. During his leadership at Yale, Rudolph created a network of international talent. There were always surprise visits by distinguished architects who would give lectures, hold impromptu crits and join juries to argue and debate with the staff and students alike.

There was a kind of missionary zeal about Rudolph as he paced the design studios, stopping to review work on the drawing boards. He could be daunting in the manner and content of his delivery—but you also knew that he was equally tough on himself. I found that out firsthand by working in his office as a lowly draughtsman. Those immaculate illustrations that I had long admired turned out to be giant-sized ink drawings on white boards—the grain of lines would be designed for later reduction in scale. I was assigned the task of upgrading a set of these drawings on a current project. Details of the perspectives would be changed by pasting over pieces of white card like a patchwork quilt and I would redraw the areas under scrutiny—matching up the thousands of handcrafted lines. Rudolph would orchestrate these images—a decision to deepen the shadows, for example, would involve new layers of extensive crosshatching. The combination of a strong work ethic and an impatience to view the end result would lead to rapid transformations of the view points for the master's judgment.

Many of these drawings, especially the perspective sections, would encapsulate in a single image the range of Rudolph's concerns as an architect. There was his quest to define and model space with light and planar surfaces—his interest in climate and the relationship between structure and services—his explorations

NORMAN FOSTER

White card model of Foster's design for an office building (1962), a project assigned by Paul Rudolph.

into modularity and the potential of prefabrication—a later interest in high-density urban megastructures.

These concerns have been shared by many architects in the past and that will continue, but Rudolph developed a very personal language out of such issues as well as the diversity of building materials that he also explored during his career. I remember that Rudolph made constant reference to the work of other architects to illustrate an issue of form or a point of theory. But his own work was never obviously derivative, however strong his points of reference or historical awareness.

His can-do mentality and a society that is less hidebound, more receptive to change, produced results that were arguably more extrovertly American than European. It is interesting that Robert Stern, who was both a student and an academic at Yale, might feel that Frank Lloyd Wright was a strong influence on Rudolph's work, and it might be difficult to think of a more American architect than Wright. But Rudolph's interest in the relationship between the old and the new and his pronouncements against the insularity of the individual building lost in a sea of cars—his plea for a larger scale urbanity of public spaces—these were surely European in their inspiration. Perhaps that is why, in his larger urban projects, he always tried to extend the fabric of the building in order to create the "place" or "plaza."

There is also a monumentality about many of his projects which, combined with the use of sculpted concrete, could be seen as linked back to the works of Le Corbusier. It is significant that conversations and writings about Rudolph often refer to Wright and Corbusier as his architect heroes with Gropius as the revered educator—again the interplay of New World and Old.

Interior of the open-plan studio of Foster and Partners.

NIGEL YOUNG/FOSTER AND PARTNERS

NIGEL YOUNG/FOSTER AND PARTNERS

Riverside (1986–90), London, England, a mixed-use development that houses the Foster and Partners studio.

Perhaps the strongest common thread that linked Paul Rudolph the architect and Paul Rudolph the teacher was a sense of absolute commitment, a moral imperative in which no effort was spared, however late in the process, to improve the quality of architecture, whether in his own buildings or by inspiration in the work of his students. It is an example that will live on in all of those who shared his influence.

In 1998, nearly forty years after my graduation, I contributed to a seminar in London on the special relationship between America and Britain with Yale as a point of reference. I spoke about my time as a student in New Haven—how I enjoyed living next to the school as a fellow of Jonathan Edwards College, whose garden courtyard formed a link to the Yale Art Gallery by Louis I. Kahn. At that time the architecture studios were located on the top floor of this building, and I was deeply impressed that they were open day and night—a welcome relief from the European hours and attitudes I had left behind in Manchester.

As I described this environment to the audience in the seminar I realized that in so many ways it was a word picture of the way that I lived and worked at Riverside—the site of my present practice on the bank of the Thames in London. The studio there is open twenty-four hours a day, seven days a week, and I live above it with an entrance through the courtyard!

Mario Gandelsonas

on

Mies van der Rohe

FIRST ENCOUNTER: I am working as an intern in the early 1960s on a small cubic crypt to be located in an exclusive area of the Olivos cemetery near Buenos Aires. It is an eight-foot Miesian cube, an elementary steel structure with translucent marble infill panels. There are long discussions around the resolution of the corners. Blurred yet poignant, these traces mark my first encounter with the American Mies—my introduction to the difficult yet determined practice of crafting elementary form from a syntax of ready-made steel L and I beams.

Second encounter: I am walking down Park Avenue in the fall of 1968. Mies's Seagram Building produces a discontinuity in the linearity of the street, a punctuation it still performs for me thirty years later despite the confusion produced by its neighbors: the second-rate, Miesian-influenced structures that inhabit its immediate context. By day the building's vertical recession from the street wall and horizontal break with the ground combine with the relentless rhythm of its façade and the luxurious materiality of its understated marble floors and bronze skin to create dazzling effect. By night it becomes a phantasmal presence, a dark figure hovering above the refined glow of its lobby and silhouetted against the background of its fabriclike back.

These two encounters with the American Mies, the first mediated through a work influenced by him, the second a direct experience of one of his masterpieces, have left indelible marks on my reading of his work. The American Mies I first encountered, the postmodernist architect of urban buildings, became the point of departure for a retroactive discovery of the earlier German Mies, the modernist architect of isolated houses and exhibition pavilions. This temporal reversal prompted an alternative to the standard interpretation of his work. Mies's work has always been divided into two stages. The first, the German stage, is marked by the radical exploration of a "universal space," a space that broke with the classical past, dissolved the box, and sent planes trailing into the landscape. The second, the American stage, is characterized by an architectural research into buildings that repudiated "stylishness" and willful innovation.

PREVIOUS SPREAD: **Seagram Building by Mies van der Rohe, New York City, 1958.**

However, while the standard view interprets the American stage as focused on elementary volume, skin, and structure, that is, the Mies of my first encounter, it disregards the implications of the Mies of my second. Missing from this view are the various relationships that Mies established between architecture and the city: the opening of architecture to urban forces and configurations, the opposition between background fabric and foreground object, and the accommodation of the different speeds of urban viewing—the careful scrutiny of the pedestrian architectural connoisseur versus the quick glance of the lay driver. The effects of these relationships can be seen in Mies's willingness to operate within the most stringent programmatic limitations (speculative office and apartment buildings) and in his simultaneous obsession with detail, the building's elegant "slow read," and overall form, the building's immediate legibility to those observers travelling at high speed.

Read in their urban dimension, Mies's buildings and compositional strategies (in particular the European Mies) have become entry points for the establishment of a critical reading of modernism within our work. In the attempt to blur modernist oppositions this reading proposes the development of new configurations and the construction of new symbolic structures within contemporary architecture. Working throughout various scales and programs, this reading is particularly manifest in three projects designed by Agrest and Gandelsonas in the last ten years: an interior on Central Park West in New York; a gate for Cranbrook College,

PAUL WARCHOL

Central Park West duplex interior by Gandelsonas, New York City, 1987–88.

and a town for ten thousand people in The People's Republic of China.

The interior on Central Park West transforms what was once for Mies a modernist critique of the dialectics of classical space into a critique of modernism itself. Taking the Miesian pinwheel plan and turning it back on itself, the interior calls into question three important oppositions within modernism: plan versus volume, field versus room, and solid versus void. Upon entry, a staircase introduces the viewer to the compositional theme, a circular movement implied in plan. Once inside, a pinwheel organization of thick walls establishes a field of action while simultaneously suggesting a sequence of rooms. Thick inhabitable walls question the opposition between plan and volume, solid and void, while metaphorically relocating the American urban landscape within the interior—a site where the distinction between fabric and objects has been blurred for quite some time. At the level of detail, luxurious materials are juxtaposed with plain, molding with reveal, to blur the opposition between classical versus modernist detailing, concealing versus revealing.

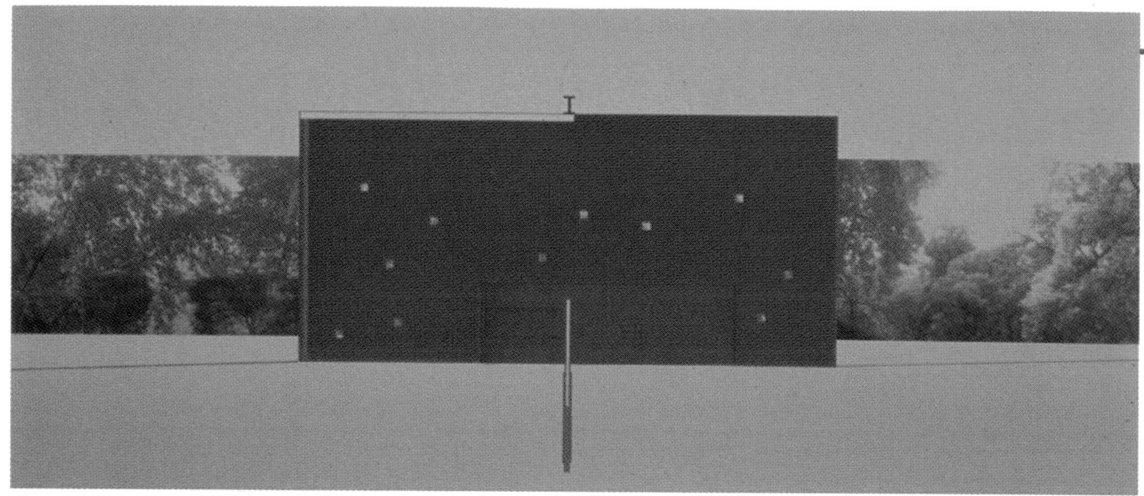

AGREST & GANDELSONAS ARCHITECTS

AGREST & GANDELSONAS ARCHITECTS

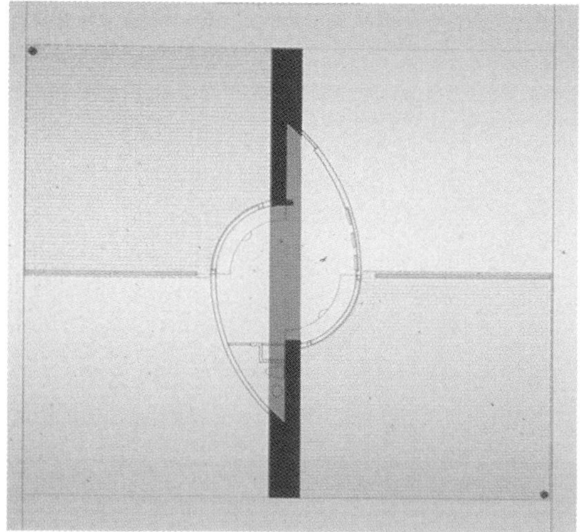

AGREST & GANDELSONAS ARCHITECTS

ABOVE: **View from the car gate, Cranbrook Academy, Bloomfield Hills, Michigan, 1991–92.** LEFT: **Plan gate, Cranbrook Academy.** BELOW LEFT: **Orientation elevation gate, Cranbrook Academy.**

It would best be said that Mies has entered our work not through visual transposition but at a formal and discoursive level. Although the Cranbrook campus could be at first interpreted as following Mies's dictum "making architecture with structure only," the configuration of plan and section are determined by the formal development of questions inherent in the program. The Cranbrook Gate is a symmetrical project that suppresses centrality to emphasize peripheral movement—its center is inhabited by a wall that separates two oppositional lanes of vehicular traffic. The form is thus an effect of a double movement and the control of this movement at the campus edge. Two virtual cubes are implied by a structure that articulates four basic architectural elements: the brick wall, the round column, the I beam, the flat roof.

In the project for a town for ten thousand people in The People's Republic of China, an L building in plan and section produces the basic structure of the project: a three-dimensional, Z-configured building. The Z buildings, in a critique of the lack of section in the extruded plans of the German Mies, read alternatively as low-rise, high-rise, or "horizontal skyscraper" (El Lissitsky). The alternating rhythm of their location (framing the street with the low-rise section or marking the corners with the high-rise towers) produces a shifting ground, alternately read as an extruded fabric or a field filled with objects. The aim of the project is to produce precisely an undecidable urban spatial condition, to blur the opposition between fabric and object. The project also produces an indeterminate temporal situation by projecting overlaps within the three different stages of the town's development: (1) dense low-rise fabric, (2) very large building objects, and (3) a mix of Z-shaped low-rise fabric with small towers that acts as a link between the other two. The Shanghai plan also radicalizes the double condition driver versus pedestrian, slow movement versus fast speed, at work in the Seagram building in New York.

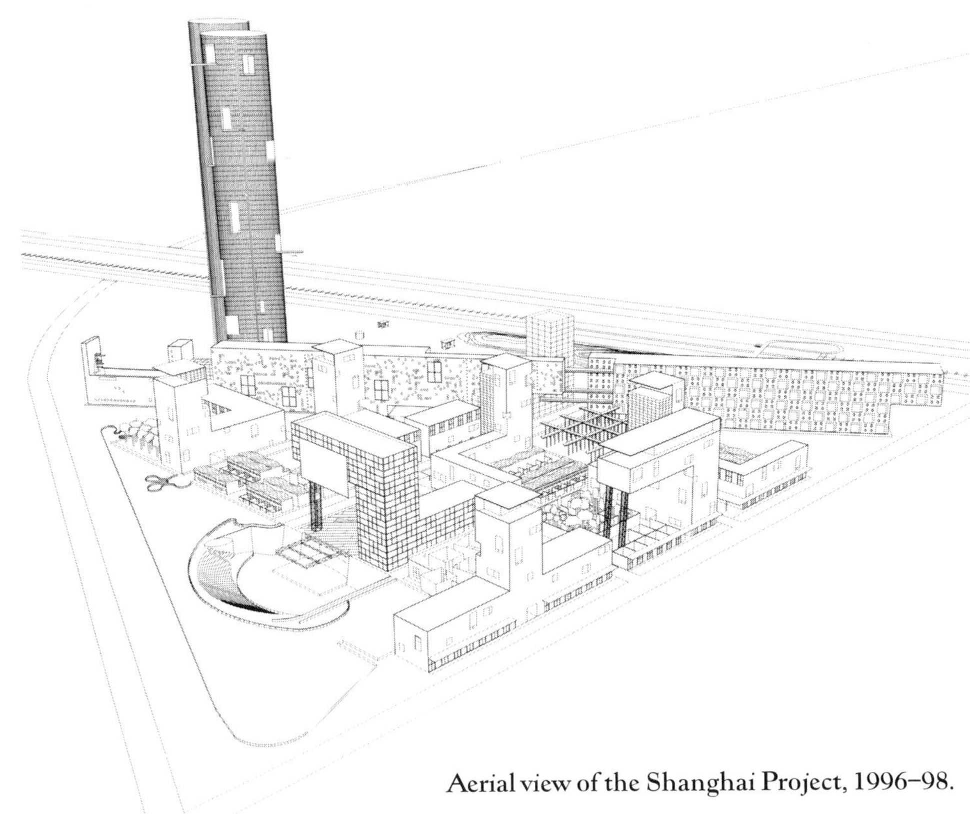

Aerial view of the Shanghai Project, 1996–98.

AGREST & GANDELSONAS ARCHITECTS

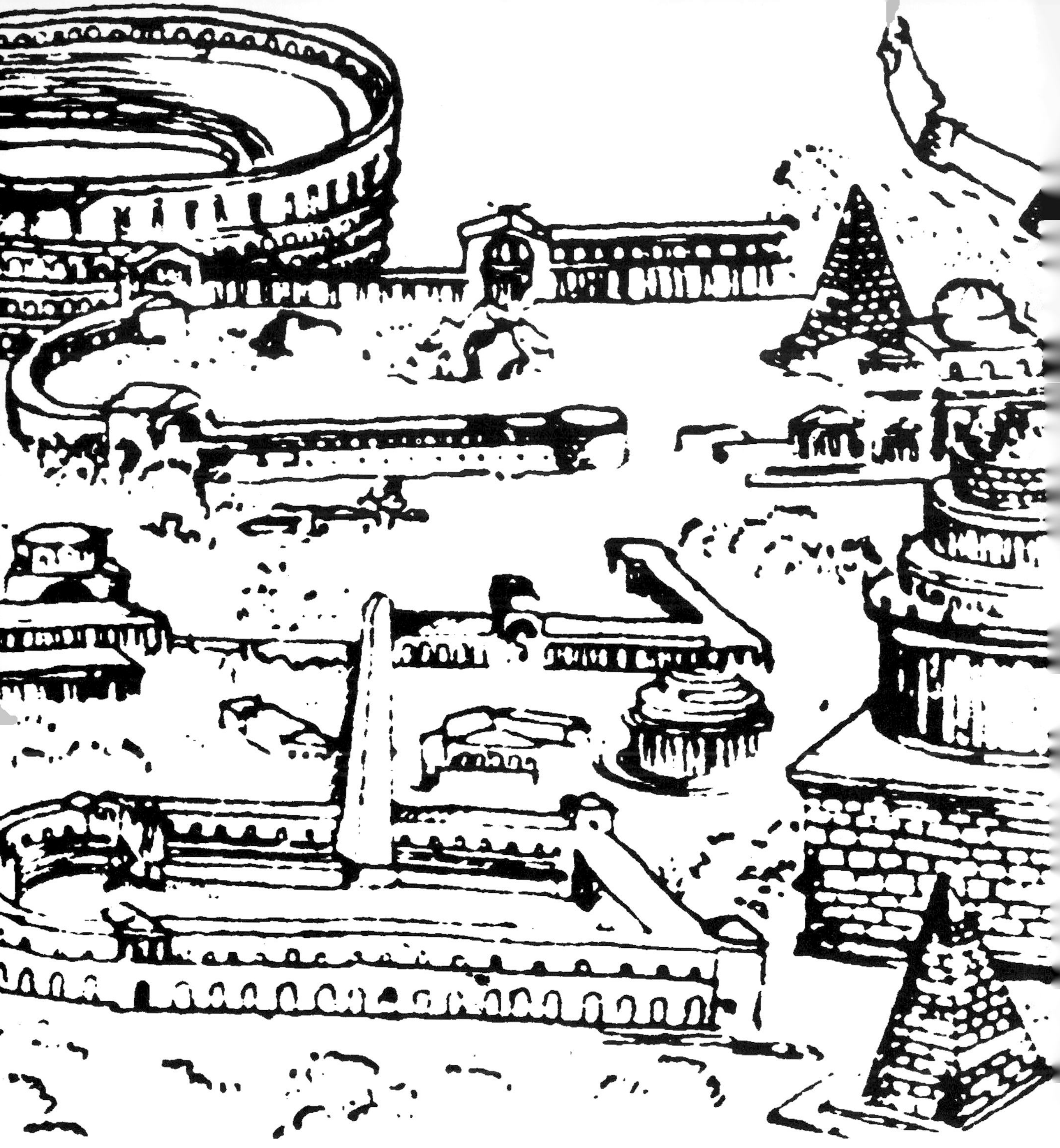

Drawing by Le Corbusier depicting several isolated monuments of ancient Rome.

Michael Graves *on* Le Corbusier

DRAWING FOR ME IS a fundamental act of an architectural thought process. Drawing is in part a mnemonic device, a kind of visual diary. However, because of the intrinsic reciprocity between mind and act, drawing goes beyond simple information. It fixes in our inner experience what we have seen. As an essential part of the conception of architecture, as well as of painting and sculpture, it is also conjectural or speculative in nature and therefore exists at the heart of the creative process.

Le Corbusier, who repeatedly published his travel sketches and even the crudest of his project studies, was exemplary in considering drawing as a "conscience." We customarily value sketches for their sensual, impressionistic qualities, but the appeal of Le Corbusier's drawings rests largely on the inquiry they record: his search for what he considered a rational basis for architecture.

I was originally encouraged to enter the field of architecture because of my interest in drawing. As students, my classmates and I pored over the published drawings and buildings of other architects, and in graduate school at Harvard, the work and writings of Le Corbusier assumed the most prominent position in our self-education. There was scarcely a colleague of mine who did not know the *Oeuvre Complete* by heart. I found it interesting that my fellow students would examine in detail the volume representing Corb's work from 1910–29 to discern the differences between his wonderful black and white photographs and his drawings. I never thought for a moment that they were supposed to match! Rather, it appeared to me that the drawings held ideas about architecture broader and more fundamental than the information about the specific project at hand.

Le Corbusier himself leads us to that conclusion through propositions such as "The Lessons of Rome." His small drawing depicting isolated monuments of antique Rome is accompanied by a series of geometric objects abstracted from that urban landscape. It is fascinating to me that Le Corbusier's drawings reveal a broad knowledge of the "literature" of drawings by others. This very sketch of Rome in fact was derived from a 1561 engraving by Pirro Ligorio, who likewise projected from ancient ruins the geometric essence of Roman monuments.

Le Corbusier, like Pirro Ligorio, required himself to see the archetypal condition of historical artifacts and thus avoided being trapped by contextual and often nostalgic representations. We also know from

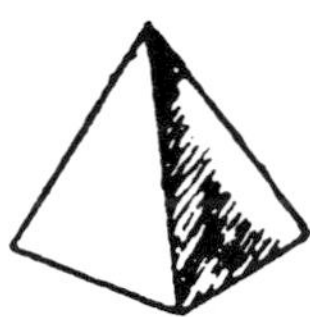
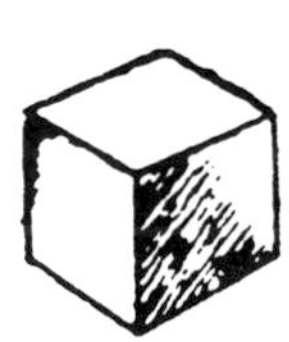

Drawing by Le Corbusier of pure geometric forms.

COURTESY OF MICHAEL GRAVES

"Archaic Landscape," gouache painting by Michael Graves, 1993.

COURTESY OF MICHAEL GRAVES & ASSOCIATES

TIMOTHY HURSLEY

ABOVE: Graves's Denver Central Library, Denver, Colorado: drawing of the south elevation, pencil and colored pencil on yellow tracing paper, 1993. RIGHT: The Denver Central Library, Denver, Colorado: detail photograph of the south façade and rotunda. BELOW: Kasumi Research and Training Center, Tsukuba City, Japan.

his built work that being able to see these objects in their pure state in turn allowed him to reassemble them in combination. Le Corbusier understood the rational basis for architecture first and then developed the specific or local manifestation.

From early on, these exercises in revealing the underlying basis of architectural composition greatly influenced my thinking and what I chose to record in my sketch books for later use. I too became interested in the combinations of forms as they begin to suggest the development of architecture. For example, in one of my paintings of an archaic landscape, the way a block and a column supports an overhead plane becomes a way of framing, even a portal. (Le Corbusier's work has many examples of this combination.) These elemental combinations are abstract and speculative, to be sure, but begin to suggest that there is a formal language of architecture that shapes our understanding of our surroundings. In projects of mine such as the Denver Central Library and Kasumi's Research and Training Center in Japan, I composed the buildings as combinations of individual elements, each with both a formal and a programmatic purpose.

In addition to the interests in formal composition, Le Corbusier's drawings and buildings contain narrative or symbolic references that are fascinating to discover. One of my favorites is a very charming group of drawings of the second project for a villa for Mme. Meyer. Le Corbusier takes us on a promenade through a series of interiors and ends up at the roof terrace where a convivial lunch is displayed like a Cubist still life. He asks us to look out through his architectural frame toward a curious ruin in the landscape, a miniature temple within the concavity of a rustic rock mountain. (This same theme can be found in the paintings of Poussin, Chatelet, and de Chirico.) As in his other work, Le Corbusier insists that we understand both the external figure of the geometric solid of the mountain and the hollowed-out volume, the space. In the portal of the mock mountain at Villa Meyer, Le Corbusier sees the primary solids assembled in their elemental forms—plinth, column, and pediment—which allows us to distinguish their individual meanings and characteristics. Thus the rite of passage through his villa journey is made symbolically complete by the suggestion of return to the landscape, made vivid by a memorable historic reference.

The study of drawings and drawing as an investigative process are for me, as they were for Le Corbusier, an essential part of both design and teaching others about architecture. I was always struck by the phrase Le Corbusier used to instruct young architects when he asked them to "trace the lines." (My version of that concept has been the basis of my teaching in design studios at Princeton for over thirty years.) By that, Le Corbusier meant, among other things, that to get to know plans and, by extension, to learn how to make a plan, one should trace the lines of plans by others, say, for example, those contained in Letarouilly's nineteenth-century chronicle of buildings in Rome, itself a documentation of precedent. By tracing the lines, we not only come to know in detail how the various rooms work together, but also identify the *parti*, the underlying conceptual organi-

HIROKAZU YOKOSE

Drawing by Le Corbusier for his second project for a villa for Mme. Meyer.

zation. While poets and musicians have their own ways of remembering phrases and even whole scores, architects I think are better served by drawing and redrawing as a way of remembering. And in the process, the insight we gain about the *parti* allows us to understand the creative thinking and not just memorize the moves. In Le Corbusier's 1960 book, *Creation Is a Patient Search*, subtitled *A Self-Portrait*, he describes drawing as a continuum: observing—discovering—inventing—creating.[1] Through drawing our observations, I believe we discover the conceptual nature of the architecture, which in turn becomes the basis for our own creative inquiries.

As the recipient of the 1960 Rome Prize, I was fortunate to be able to spend two years at the American Academy in Rome, where I devoted much of my time to drawing and studying architectural precedents in Italy and elsewhere in Europe. The influence of Le Corbusier was constantly on my mind. One September, I took a side trip to the Rhone Valley in France and sketched the church of St. Etienne at Nevers. On the same trip, I visited Le Corbusier's recently completed Convent of La Tourette near Lyons and made a drawing of it too. (Now that I typically carry around pocket-sized sketchbooks, those drawings in retrospect were a little too large—40 × 28 inches!) When I returned to Rome and looked at the work from my trip, I found a striking similarity in the way that space was held in those two drawings. Rather boldly and presumptuously, I sent the two drawings to Le Corbusier and of course never heard from him. For years, I thought that he tossed them out or that they simply never arrived at his office.

Much later, a friend of mine doing research at the Fondation Le Corbusier in Paris called and asked, "Michael, how did two drawings of yours come to be included in Corb's archives?" I sheepishly told her the story. She told me that the two drawings were catalogued and filed in a rather prominent position, no doubt because of their enormous size.

In looking at copies of these drawings recently, I was immediately drawn back into the original inquiry, a recollection of my inner experience. Despite the striking difference in style and scale of these two buildings, I had discovered a similarity in their underlying spatial characteristics. The framing of the views into the two churches allowed me to discover fundamental aspects of their plans, where the spatial sequence is understood as part procession and part resistance or denial. It was through the act of drawing—tracing the lines, as Le Corbusier would say—that I became engaged in the architecture and in its underlying creative process.

1 Le Corbusier [pseudo], *Creation Is a Patient Search*, translated by James Palmes (New York: Frederick A. Praeger, Inc., 1960) 201.

COURTESY OF MICHAEL GRAVES

ABOVE: **Charcoal drawing on paper by Michael Graves of Convent Sainte-Marie de la Tourette near Lyons.** BELOW: **Charcoal drawing on paper of Church of St. Etienne at Nevers by Michael Graves.**

Vittorio Gregotti

on

Peter Behrens

IN 1958, WITH MY limited German, I started studying the question of what the Expressionist movement represented within the framework of the Modern. The obstacles in that period were considerable: psychological ones, first of all, on account of the dark shadows that surrounded a cultural area (for me in a manner both fascinating and repelling) that had had many tangencies with some aspects of Nazism, a past that German historians of architecture had the tendency to place in parentheses; obstacles concerning the critical literature on the matter: In those years no study existed on the subject, and the original texts were difficult to find, and not only in Italy; and finally, obstacles of a critical historical nature. It was a matter, first and foremost, of defining whether an Expressionist architecture existed or whether Expressionism was definable rather as a moment, an aura, a feeling with different meanings, through which many German architects of the first thirty years of the century, of different origins and with different ideals, had passed. After all, as is well known, even the Expressionist movements in painting, such as the Brücke or the Blaue Reiter, had greatly differing ideal hypotheses. What relations did they have with the other movements of the first two decades of the century, from the Neue Sachlichkeit to the Novembergruppe, from the Gläserne Kette to Rationalism itself? All are critical questions, many of which today, forty years later, have found answers in the numerous studies that subsequently appeared in quick succession.

As regards my career as an architect, that research gave me the opportunity to study various protagonists, from Wilhelm Kreis to Hans Poelzig, from Erich Mendelsohn to the Gerson brothers, and among these the personality of Peter Behrens, on whom Tillmann Buddensieg and his team of researchers were to write authoritatively in the 1960s. All were personalities who had been excluded from the classic texts of the history of contemporary architecture or else had occupied a marginal position in them.

The fascination that the personality of Behrens exercised over me certainly exceeds the appreciation that I have for his works as a whole. They are certainly very discontinuous, even if I consider that the group of AEG's buildings—especially the Kleinmotoren-Fabrik and the lobby of Fahrben Industrie, with its sharp colors that bring out the vibration of the brick walls, or the Obenausen steelworks—are absolute masterpieces of this century.

In 1959, together with Aldo Rossi, I went on a

PREVIOUS SPREAD: **Behrens's Gasworks, East Harbour, Frankfurt-am-Main, Germany, 1912. View of water tower and tanks.**

ABOVE LEFT: **Behrens's Good Hope Company's office, stores, and warehouse, Oberhausen, Germany, 1921–25.**

LEFT: **Behrens's design sketch for the opening in the former Jägerstrasse, Berlin, 1927.**

Design submitted by Behrens that won the competition for reconstruction of Alexander Platz, Berlin, 1928–29. View onto the Rathaustrasse.

trip through Germany (with the spiritual guidance of some scholarly friends of mine—Ingeborg Bachmann and Enrico Filippini, Husserl's translator into Italian) in search of the remains of the Expressionist monuments in Hamburg, Frankfurt, Düsseldorf, Hanover, and Berlin, to prepare the special issue of *Casabella* that was to be published the following year. This was also the visit on which I met with the buildings of Peter Behrens. It was on that occasion that I became acquainted with O.M. Ungers, who was perhaps the only German architect in that period to be interested in the problem of Expressionism in architecture. The fascination of Germany, of its history between the Weimar Republic and the collective folly of Nazism, a Germany undone, divided, and its sense of guilt, the empty and tragic heart of Europe, was in those years a question both frightening and fascinating, not only for Italians emerging from Fascism, but for the culture of the whole of Europe. We architects were also interested in articulating the traditions of the Modern and its questions in a broader manner and without prejudices. Peter Behrens represented these questions and the contradictions that derived from them in an exemplary manner. He had lived near Walther Rathenau, Georg Siemmel, Max Weber, and Karl Ernst Osthaus, intellectuals who were also examining the idea of the meaning of the modern city and large-scale industry as the expression of the creative capacities of work, a commitment to an "ethics of social responsibility," and as a community, a model for possible collective democratic development that then had to witness the alliance of this same industry with Nazism and with the war. It is through the common culture of these principles with some of his major clients that the construction of works fundamental to the tradition of the Modern, such as those produced for AEG, was possible. In my view Behrens was not only one of the great precursors of modernity, who had been able to reconcile the great profession and his interest for the avant-garde, to exercise a charm that had attracted men such as Le Corbusier,

Mies van der Rohe, and Gropius to his studio, to build great monuments and persuade the representatives of major industrial powers to take decisive steps towards modernity. Above all, he also was a great artist capable of placing the contradictions of a whole culture at the center of his own work.

I must confess that I have always had great admiration not only for those people in Europe, in the generation of Peter Behrens—from Perret to Berlage, from Van de Velde to Tony Garnier—but also in the United States of Richardson and Sullivan, who took on the responsibility for making the tools and the tradition of the great profession available to modernity, to act as a medium between them and the ideas of the avant-garde. Of course, this interest of mine also corresponds to the defining for me of the limits of a tradition of the Modern in which I feel I am a participant. It has helped me to construct my work as an architect as a positive criticism of modernity, to conceive modernity itself as a structurally incomplete project capable of asking profound questions of itself and of modifying itself starting from its own bases, and to practice my work as an organic part of my life.

Furthermore, Peter Behrens's best buildings have always had, in my eyes, the fascination of the great tectonic construction, the sense of integrity of the organism at the moment of its reinvention, at the same time expressing the grandiose sentiment of collectivity, and particularly of the collectivity of work, committed to resolving every problem, respecting above all the ethics of work itself and therefore the rules of the work.

The fact that his buildings possess the capacity to maintain themselves well over time is only the technical aspect of the reasons for the choices of ma-

ANDREA MARTIRADONNA

OPPOSITE: **Color sketch of the large entrance hall to Behrens's Technology Headquarters, IG Farben Hoechst Dyeworks Administration and Research Building, Hoechst, Germany, 1920.** RIGHT: **Detail of Gregotti's Environmental Science Building at the Università degli Studi (1969–90), Palmero at the Parco d'Orléans (Gregotti & Pollini).**

terials and the details that, without exhibition, are always necessarily subject to the general meaning of the built organism. Much more important is the idea of duration that is connected with his constructions, as the capacity of architecture to bear witness to a sociohistorical condition: works committed to becoming the collective element of reference with the stability of their own expressive conditions.

Behrens's architecture restores the whole sense of the specificity of a historical tradition without this merely becoming nostalgia, memory, or a form of legitimization. On the contrary, it is on the terrain constituted by it that he builds. The way in which tradition stands alongside modernity forms its premise. The continuity of history is not refused and its presence constitutes the condition for establishing a critical dialogue with it, at a distance. The quality of his architecture is the way of occupying that distance, of setting the differences essential to the construction of the necessary new.

The history of the architectures of Peter Behrens is also a history of the mutations, the oscillations, the uncertainties of this highly sound architect, but also of his capacity to return to questioning himself rad-

Cultural Center of Belém, Lisbon, Portugal, 1988–93 (Gregotti & Risco).

MIMMO JODICE

Renovation of Torre Federiciana from Piazza Madrice with remains of ancient fortification, Menfi, Italy, 1984–95.

ALBERTO MUCIACCIA

ically when faced with any problem, to attempt to give each of them a specific answer without worrying a priori about the continuity of a style, but obtaining it precisely for this reason.

A wide range of historical conditions separate us from the methods with which Peter Behrens's work has developed. Any process of stylistic imitation is impossible for us; nevertheless, I believe in the choice of an ideal maestro, of a reference to whom to go with the soul, as well as with the mind, at the moment of the constitution of the project. A maestro is all the more important, however, the more we become aware of what differentiates us from him, looking at him as a point of reference to measure the detachment, the distance that divides us as much as the line that connects us.

Exterior, Kahn's Richards Medical Research Building, University of Pennsylvania, Philadelphia, 1961.

Charles Gwathmey

on

Louis I. Kahn

WHEN I WAS A second-year undergraduate architecture student at the University of Pennsylvania in the fall of 1957, a seminal event occurred in the exhibition hall of the School of Architecture building.

It was announced in the morning that Master's Professor Louis Kahn would unveil his model for the proposed Richards Medical Research Building at Penn. In the afternoon, a white sheet–covered object on a painted plywood pedestal was placed in the center of the space, and the word spread that the model had arrived. The speculative anticipation and excitement were rampant throughout the studios, and the hall was packed by four o'clock. Nobody could wait, and nobody dared peek.

Promptly at five o'clock, "Lou" to his intimates, "Mr. Kahn" to the students, walked up to the pedestal, stood looking at the sheet, and waited for total silence. He spoke in a low raspy voice, with an intensity and passion that were mesmerizing.

The Richards Project represented a summary and culmination of his ideas about architecture to that point.

He described the ideal of the served and the service spaces as being articulate from one another, yet inherently integrated by structure and mechanical systems.

He described the ideal of structural expression as a true representation and opportunity to ennoble form and physics.

He described materiality as an obligation to render truthfully the nature of gravity, density, opacity, translucency, and transparency.

He described the logic and irrefutability of geometry as a basis for formalism, as well as programmatic expression and hierarchy.

He was poetic and compelling.

The anticipation of the removal of the sheet was unbelievable. Mr. Kahn reached up and pulled it away. There was an audible gasp, followed by absolute silence.

The solid basswood model, incredibly crafted, radiated essence. It was stunningly clear and infinitely dense, both literally and philosophically.

There was no question that we were all experiencing a unique, revelatory, and transcendent moment in architectural history, where a new idea was totally manifested and the future of twentieth-century architecture would be altered.

For me, the experience consolidated my determination, reinforced my commitment, and fueled my passion for architecture.

I never had Mr. Kahn formally as a teacher, nor did I know him. He was both aloof and seemingly unapproachable. However, I attended all of his mas-

LEFT: **Interior of Richards Medical Research Building.** OPPOSITE: **Rudolph's Art and Architecture Building, 1963, with Kahn's Yale University Art Gallery in the distance. Yale University, New Haven, Connecticut, 1953.**

FARSHID ASSASSI

Gwathmey's Levitt Center for University Advancement; southeast view as seen from the president's house, University of Iowa, Iowa City, Iowa, 1993.

ter's studio juries at Penn and his lectures over the years. His ethic, his morality, his passion, and his work never diminished. Instead, there is no question that he/it inspired, motivated, and influenced my own work.

The most memorable communication was when I asked him if I should transfer to MIT after my second year at Penn. He said to wait another year and go to Yale. I left Penn after my third year and transferred to Yale's school of architecture, whose chairman was Paul Rudolph.

Where Penn seemed insulated, removed, and dependent upon the stature of Louis Kahn and his pedagogic disciples, Yale was the opposite. Paul Rudolph was a younger master: accessible, energetic, hyperactive, and a firm believer in pluralism. The school thrived on visiting architects from all over the world. The more varied the points of view, the more dynamic the dialogue, the more opportunities for exploration, and the richer the experience.

Coincidentally, the studios were on the fourth floor of Kahn's Art Gallery Building (1951–53), another signature work that had profound influence on both the art of architecture and teaching.

In retrospect, the three years at each school was an ideal educational experience, both for Penn's singularity and Yale's variation, neither lacking in intensity.

I got to know Paul Rudolph during my first year at Yale in 1960. Many students worked in his office, helping draft his famous ink, one-point perspective sections, a prototypical documentation of his projects. During those periods, we would observe his singular struggle over the design for the Yale School of Art and Architecture Building to be located across York Street from Kahn's Art Gallery Building.

It was obvious and also very poignant that Rudolph's objective and focus was to make a greater building than Kahn's. His insecurity and compulsion were manifested in his inability to come to a finite conclusion and commitment to a design. The iterations seemed endless and the strain noticeable.

The formal *parti* remained relatively intact, but the refinement process, burdened by insistent complexities and overlays, continued to erode the initial clarity and elemental quality of the design. It seemed to all of us, observing the process, that reductive, subtractive editing would have been more productive. However, on these issues, Rudolph was incredibly sensitive and resistive to any dialogue.

The most interesting observation is that the primary, formal, and organizational parti of these two buildings, the Richards Medical Research Building and the Art and Architecture Building, designed during the same period of time, are very similar, in that both are reliant on vertical circulation towers supporting horizontal trays.

In my naive but intuitive critical perception, I understood the difference between the absolute, elemental clarity of Kahn's idea-building and Rudolph's decorated diagram. The essence of Kahn's building was diagrammatic, and Rudolph's was overwrought by complexities.

The composite experience of the unveiling of the Richards Building, the three years of working in the Yale Art Gallery and the involvement with Rudolph's process, as well as the ultimate reality of his building, was indelibly complex and meaningful. It also proved that the clarity and purity of an idea must prevail, while tangential distractions dilute both meaning and manifestation.

There has not been in modern architecture a more meteoric ascendance than Rudolph's, nor a more catastrophic rejection, based upon the realization of a single building. The Yale Art and Architecture Building, for all intents and purposes, signaled the end of his career in America and initiated the rise of postmodernism as an alternative language.

As I said, I never really knew Kahn. I loved Rudolph the man, and always admired his intellect, sensitivity, and intensity. I remained a loyal and supportive friend until his death.

However, the lessons learned from both men and their buildings were and are inseparable, indis-

FARSHID ASSASSI

Levitt Center's south façade.

pensable, and unforgettable. I am grateful, more knowledgeable, and richer, yet somewhat saddened at the same time.

Architecture is not finite, but speculative and elusive. To extend the known requires the artist to risk. Risk inherently raises the possibility of failure. However, the creative process cannot exist without either.

Kahn's Richards Building was rejected by its users immediately as being inflexible, too light, too hot, willful, and a dogmatic imposition by an arrogant architect. The same could be said for Rudolph's Art and Architecture Building.

But the singular difference historically (and by that I mean its influence and why one building changed modern architecture positively and the other did not) was in the ultimate and irrefutable vision and clarity of the idea and the reality, versus the insecurity of the same.

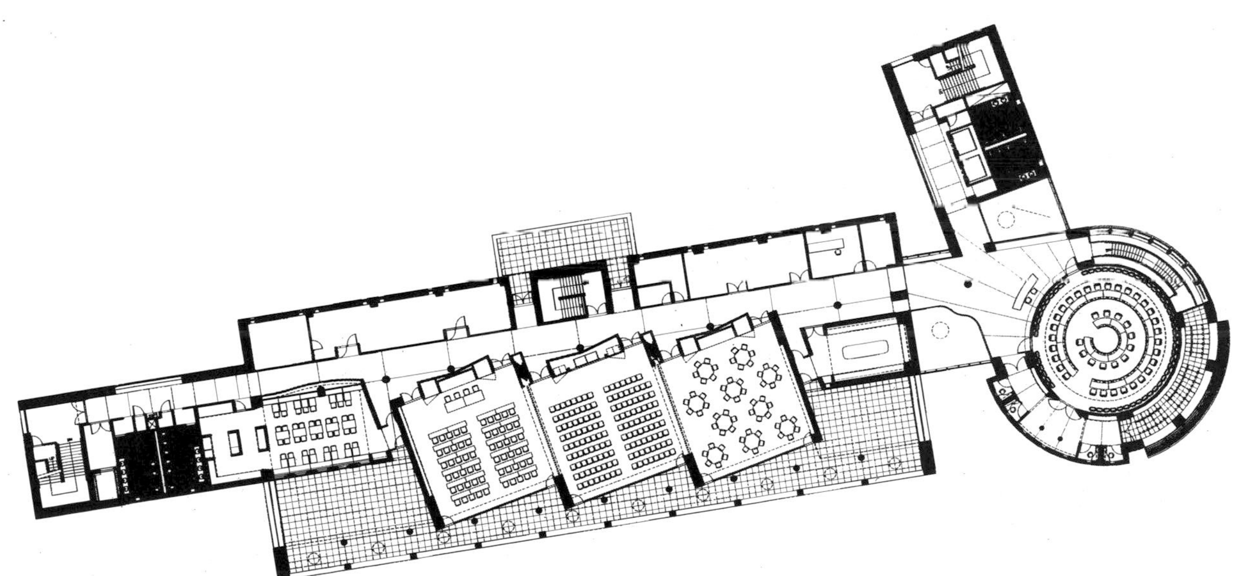

GWATHMEY SIEGEL & ASSOCIATES

ABOVE: **Rendering of street-level plan for the Levitt Center.** OPPOSITE: **Detail of the center's promenade stair.**

FARSHID ASSASSI

Hugh Hardy

on

William Van Alen

IT IS NOT POSSIBLE TO write about architecture in New York City without discussing the Chrysler Building. Its astonishing individuality is identified with the city in ways few other structures can claim, except perhaps its popular rival, the Empire State Building. While the career of the Chrysler Building's architect, William Van Alen, has no direct parallel with mine at HHPA, the revisionist spirit and iconoclastic nature of his early work show certain similarities. But it is in the Chrysler Building's extraordinary exuberance that true kinship is formed between us.

Van Alen was born in Brooklyn in 1882 and attended Pratt Institute but did not graduate. He worked for several architects as an apprentice before winning the Paris Prize

CHRIS LITTLE

CHRIS LITTLE

PREVIOUS SPREAD: **William Van Alen's Chrysler building, New York City, 1928–30.**
ABOVE: **The 2100-seat auditorium of Hardy's Alaska Center for the Performing Arts.**
ABOVE RIGHT: **Lobby of the Alaska Center for the Performing Arts.**

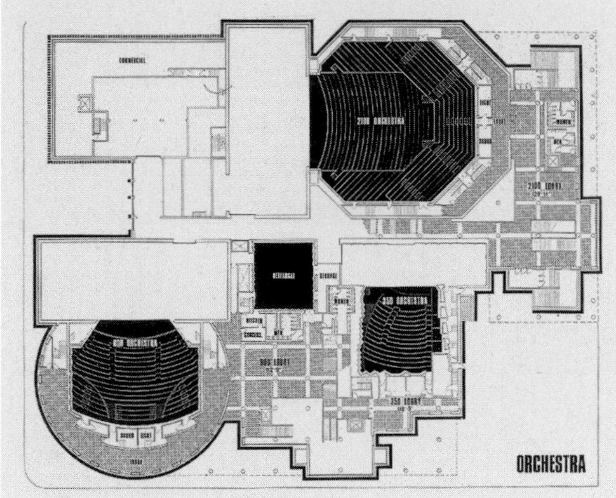

HHPA

Alaska Center for the Performing Arts, section A.

in 1908. He then studied the Beaux-Arts approach to design in the Paris atelier of M. Laloux, producing painterly designs like the *analytique* for *A Monument to be Erected on an Island in the Sea to Commemorate a Great Naval Battle*. But despite this indoctrination with Beaux-Arts stylistic tenets, he returned to New York a confirmed modernist, seeking new ways to clothe high-rise structures. In 1912 he was one of the first to design a New York building without a cornice. Although not strong in theory, Van Alen was a gifted designer who enjoyed exploring unusual fenestration patterns for retail uses and exploiting detailing opportunities offered by exterior walls that could literally be hung on steel-frame buildings.

My firm was founded in 1976 as a collaboration among three architects who shared a revisionist point of view about architecture. Our first public building, Cincinnati's Playhouse in the Park, stands outside New York, and it is distinguished, like Van Alen's early work, by an exploration of the relationship between exterior skin and interior structure. There was, however, no conscious design connection between the Chrysler Building's theatrics and our theater. In subsequent development of public buildings, HHPA designed the Alaska Center for the Performing Arts in 1988, a building whose patterned exterior and liberal use of color and texture recall the enthusiasm of Van Alen's work, but there was no conscious connection between the two.

It is possible to find the same enthusiasm for a "loose fit" between structure and cladding in much of HHPA's work, as well as a great enjoyment of decorative surfaces. The Joyce Theater, for instance, uses a deliberately Art Deco recall from the original façade of patterned brick, a four-color terrazzo entrance floor and illuminated, pattered metal fascias in the auditorium, all of which give this reconstructed space a specifically jazzy character. Even though nothing here is a direct quotation from the Chrysler Building, ebullience is clearly present.

Ironically, the one building designed by HHPA in direct response to the Chrysler Building, Riverbank West, was not built as I had intended. This speculative high-rise housing tower was imagined as a patterned essay to mark West Forty-second Street, in the hope it could complement Van Alen's masterpiece to the east. The HHPA building was to have been made of black-and-white brick, but at the insistence of the developer (who wanted a more conventional result), the exterior was changed to beige and brown, giving the tower a far more mundane appearance. How different was Van Alen's experience with Walter Chrysler, a client who kept demanding more presence, more verve.

Van Alen and his partner, H. Craig Severance, had earned considerable recognition before the Chrysler Building was built. To quote *Architectural Record* in 1924, "Among those architects who show the greatest energy in shaking off the shackles of purposeless convention are Severance and Van Alen." Similarly, when HHPA was given the Firm of the Year Award from the AIA in 1981, the citation read, "Designers of distinguished new structures, restorers of some of the finest treasures of an equally distinguished past. The success of their work is a testament to the values of experimentation and a collaborative spirit that responds with grace to the needs of a plu-

SUSAN GRAY/OVO WORKS

Stainless steel eagle gargoyle, icon of the Chrysler automobile, Van Alen's Chrysler Building, New York City, 1928–30.

ralistic society and the realities of the marketplace." Both firms practiced architecture against the grain of currently accepted aesthetic ideas, but with the exception of his stormy relationship with Walter Chrysler, Van Alen did not benefit from the collaborative design process, which has nourished HHPA.

None of Van Alen's early work prepares us for the Chrysler Building: a patterned monument of unbridled optimism. It is a singular accomplishment, demonstrating an ingenuity and bold perception unsurpassed—then or now—by any architect anywhere in the world. Its use of materials alone, black-and-white brick patterns and stainless-steel details combined with automobile imagery borrowed from Chrysler products, make it extraordinary. (HHPA has also used automobile imagery by incorporating bumpers and hoods in the walls of its auditorium for the American Film Institute at the Kennedy Center.) But just as significant is its tapered silhouette of a freestanding tower whose foursquare streetscape walls skillfully make its transition to a needled dome in the sky. Only a remarkable collaboration between architect and client could bring about such a distinctive building.

SHEILA METZNER

The Art Deco skyscraper with its metal sunburst spire.

The Chrysler Building project began with ex-Senator William H. Reynolds, a realty operator, who wanted to build the world's tallest building. He hired Van Alen, then forty years old, to design a structure forty feet taller than the Eiffel Tower's 1,000 feet. Originally conceived by Reynolds as an office building, it was about to be converted to a hotel when Walter P. Chrysler purchased the lease and the architect's design (although subsequent disagreement between Van Alen and Chrysler resulted in a lawsuit on the matter). The building was originally imagined with a helmetlike top, but when a race with Forty Wall Street for height supremacy became a paramount concern for Chrysler, the top's design was changed to its present, renowned, needled profile. This exuberance subsequently forced the Empire State to add an illuminated, dirigible mast as the price of claiming title as the world's tallest building. Early sketches by Van Alen show a horizontal division at the shaft's apex before it culminated in a series of setbacks ending in a traditional dome. It is obvious that Chrysler's ambitions and his demand to redesign yielded a more notable result. As a result of Chrysler's urging, Van Alen's signature peak represents a progression from rectangular to triangular windows radiating patterns that move upward in semicircular setbacks of ribbed stainless steel, all of this capped by a slender spire that pierces the sky 1,048 feet in the air.

Once Van Alen had learned how to aesthetically divorce the skin of a high-rise building from its structural frame, all sorts of aesthetic games became possible. His decorative patterns on the outside both recognize and ignore the interior structure of the building. Although he emphasizes verticality in the three central window bays, black-and-white horizontal brick stripes pattern the corners, acknowledging the differences in weight-bearing properties between the building's central columns and its corner structural system. Because light and air had to be provided naturally, and not distributed mechanically, the lower floors' configuration required an inset portion of the plan to permit perimeter ventilation. Van Alen takes advantage of this requirement to make a dramatic gesture and brings the central shaft down to within four stories of the street.

The Chrysler Building is clearly of its time and an immediately recognizable example of 1920s exuberance, but what continues to make it so compelling? How does it so successfully capture the spirit of New York? Contemporary accounts did not quite know what to make of this zestful stranger, set amid the sober masonry towers of midtown. Van Alen was denounced and admired as the Ziegfeld of the profession. The sober *Architectural Forum* noted in 1930, "No, the Chrysler Tower should not be criticized from the usual point of view of architectural design. It stands by itself, something apart and alone. It is simply the realization, the fulfillment in metal and masonry, of a one-man dream, a dream of such ambition and such magnitude as to defy the comprehension and the criticism of ordinary men or by ordinary standards."

SUSAN GRAY/OVO WORKS

Detail of the Chrysler Building's brick and steel cladding.

Surely the appeal of Van Alen's tower lies in an iconoclastic approach to high-rise building design. Rather than convey a staid layering of history or an earnest structural expression behind a transparent skin,

CHRIS LITTLE

Night view looking into lobby space of Hardy's Alaska Center for the Performing Arts.

this iconic office building goes for broke, flaunting the exterior skin's independence as a costume pageant of pattern, gleaming profiles, and symbolic panache. It's a theatrical gesture that identifies this as a building like no other, and gives New Yorkers proof that they are extraordinary. While the interiors, with their superb craftsmanship and exotic materials, are a matchless domain of sophisticated American modernist design, it is the exterior that most captures the imagination, making midtown not only a place of business but also a realm of romantic fantasy celebrating the ideas of wealth and industrial power. It conveys the authority of a showman at center stage, one who persuades each member of the audience that he is performing just for him or her. In Chrysler, Van Alen found a client who loved publicity and longed to make his mark in the 1920s headlong rush for height. However acrimonious their final relationship, their complementary talents produced something all its own.

There is a difference between looking for an immediate stylistic correspondence between the work of HHPA and the Chrysler Building and recognizing how kindred spirits can relate over time. The same brio that encouraged Van Alen to explore more adventuresome forms of enclosure can be found in the new Whitaker Center, in Harrisburg, Pennsylvania. Here, a heavily textured stone exterior is set against a rotated, patterned box clad in three colors of slate. Although nothing like it can be directly found in the Chrysler Building's design, the affinity is clear.

All architects fear the ignominy into which Van Alen disappeared. The Great Depression, the subsequent legal bout with Chrysler, and the lack of similar commissions severely curtailed his career. Few professionals have had to survive under such harsh economic conditions. Whether a more flexible, collaborative approach to design and management would have prevented his professional demise is unknown, but the degree to which the Chrysler Building was identified with him may have influenced potential clients to seek simpler, more spare designs from other architects. By the 1930s his title, "the Ziegfeld of the profession," had begun to work against him.

By contrast, the diversity of project type and design approach in HHPA's work has been deliberately pursued to avoid identity with any specific building type or stylistic point of view about architecture. We therefore undertake a wide range of projects, from restoration or additions to existing buildings to deliberately contemporary, freestanding structures. It is our hope that it is their spirit, not their similarity, which distinguishes the works of HHPA.

Although Van Alen lived until 1954, the year I graduated from college, nothing else in his body of work can compare with the Chrysler Building. It remains a completely original and peerless piece of architecture. By contrast, no single structure can so successfully summarize HHPA's approach to design. Instead, the diversity of our work must stand as the measure of our intent. Perhaps some future client will emerge and permit us to create an iconic, New York building, one that celebrates the vitality and daring of this city. Currently we have a second opportunity to complete a black-and-white high-rise structure with construction of Theater Row Tower on West Forty-second Street. This forty-story tower is patterned with horizontal strips of black-and-white brick. Less dynamic in form and more of an extension than Van Alen's masterpiece, this tower gently responds to its exuberance.

Let the prosaic buildings of midtown make more money; here is proof of an industrial titan's desire to strut his stuff in public amid the trophies of America's premier marketplace. It's a bravura performance, one Van Alen made possible, and one that future generations will continue to applaud vigorously, giving heart to all who challenge convention.

Arata Isozaki *on* Le Corbusier

JAQUELINE SALMON

Le Corbusier's Convent Sainte-Marie de la Tourette, Eveux, France, 1954.

Eros of the Sea

I CAN'T FORGET ONE particular snapshot: a man, seen from behind, in front of an infinitely expanding horizontal line—the Mediterranean. Facing the ocean, the old man in the swimming suit is approaching the water almost jumping, maybe dancing, on the hot burning pebbles. Whether he afterwards picked up a burning pebble or plunged into the fast current of the unexpectedly cold ocean no longer matters.

This picture, taken by Lucien Hervê, is of Le Corbusier himself. Unlike the image he projected in most other portraits—the straight-faced dandy with a pair of round, black framed eyeglasses and a bow tie—in this snapshot he was caught unwittingly in an absent-minded, unguarded posture, almost as if he were lost in nature. Perhaps in about ten more steps he would be embraced by the ocean of Mediterranean blue, backlit and glittering under the sun. He would jump into the swaying ocean, into that amorphous, continuous, adhesive, translucent substance. In the late summer of 1965, his corpse was found on the beach of Roque-Cap-Martin.

This end must not have been a mere accident, whereby the bodily functions just cease. He must have simply tried to be embraced by the sea, alone. I feel I realize that at the moment the end arrived, this old man's whole body experienced bliss as it became fully saturated by the swaying ocean. I dare to say this not only because he wrote in his diary that he was a man of space, not only spiritually but also physically, that he loved airplanes and ships and that he loved oceans, beaches, and plains more than mountains, but also because as I stood in a place totally unrelated to the sea—in the substantial darkness of a monastery standing solitarily in the woods in a corner of a swaying grass–covered plain in the middle of France—a sudden inspiration came to me. For Le Corbusier, the sea was the substance of motive force that provoked all of his imagination by permeating every detail of his body. The space of the monastery contains a sheer darkness like the deepest reaches of the sea, totally indescribable and seductive, as if it, too, would irresistibly draw us into it.

I do not know precisely when Le Corbusier, who was born in La Chaux-de-Fonds in the middle of the Swiss Alps, began to frequent the Mediterranean. But I at least know that in the last chapter of his early text, *Decorative Arts Today*, his autobiographical confession, he describes his architectural inspiration as having come from his trip to the south: Istanbul, Thessalonica, Athens, and Rome. This revelation was his perception that architecture was an art of gigantic form presented in light, and a system to express spirit. I believe that this "light" was nothing but the sun of the Mediterranean, and this architect, who early in his career preferred spaces with a clear and distinct order, later sought to draw the drama of light and shadow.

In *Purism*, a collaboration with Amédée Ozenfant, Le Corbusier persisted in pure form by rejecting all supplements: the cube, cone, sphere, cylinder, and pyramid were all primordial forms whose structures appeared in the light. The forms were clear and easy to grasp. They were unambiguous, so that they were beautiful, and the most beautiful ones at that. Then in a leap of faith he determined that the Pyramids, the Parthenon, the Colosseum, Hagia Sophia, and Brunelleschi's work were architecture because of their use of primordial forms. Where did this logic come from? He acknowledged the influence of two architects in coming to his definition—Phidias and Michaelangelo—they who intuitively concretized the theory of primary forms and mathematical harmony that Alberti attempted to elaborate in his *Ten Books of Architecture*. Isn't this early logic similar to the transparent space dominated by the absolute beauty of primary form as proposed by Plato in

OPPOSITE: **Isozaki's Team Disney building, Buena Vista, Florida, 1990.**

YASUHIRO ISHIMOTO

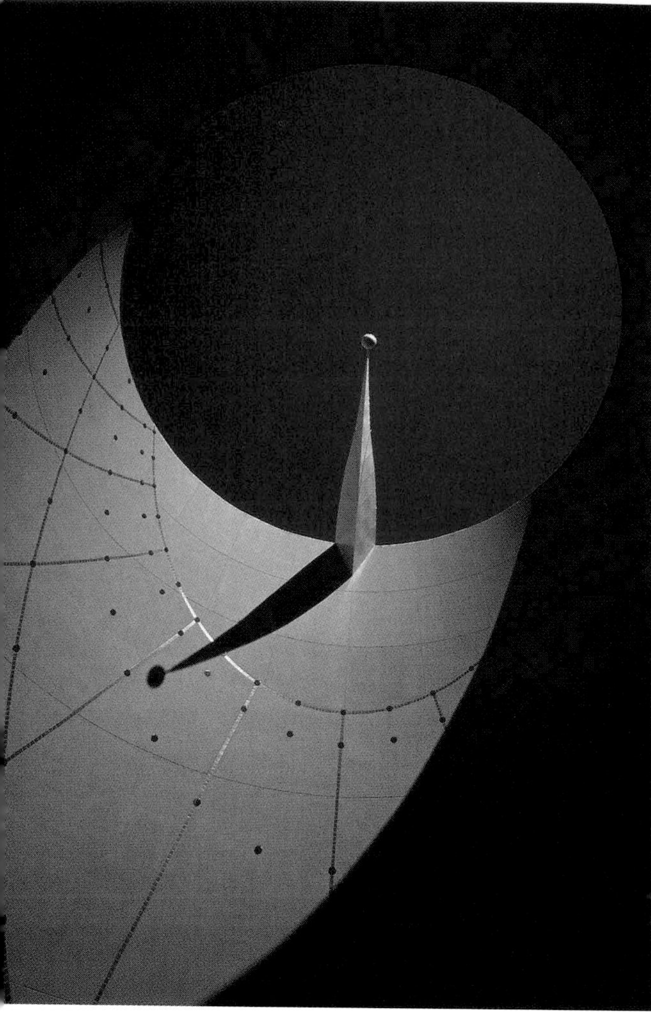

YASUHIRO ISHIMOTO

Sundial of the Team Disney building.

Philebus? "The beauty of figures is not what most people would understand. . . not the beauty of a living creature or a picture. . . something straight, or round, and the surfaces and solids which a lathe, or a carpenter's rule and square, produces from the straight and the round. . . Things like that are beautiful, not like most things, in a relative sense."[1]

This inclination is evident in the space of the architect's paintings, where transparent pure forms interpenetrate. The opaque and muddy shadows disappear, and somewhat boring figures of wine bottles and violins persist. At the time he was having his serious portraits taken in those clumsy black-framed eyeglasses with sunken eyes and thin lips, the point of his work was to produce the classical law of harmony out of new products—airplanes, ships, and silos—by identifying the machine with the Parthenon. His idea was based upon Platonic logic, yet by adding transparency he attempted to reach a more ultimate purity of form.

Suddenly, however, a shadow began to cross his architectural world. The shadow appears, for instance, in the random rubble of the base of the staircase at the Swiss Student Center, a curved accumulation of irregular stones. That is to say, the standardized, stable, transparent materials of steel, stucco, and glass, were invaded by an inexplicable, raw, opaque material. It should be said that the rough surface of the piled stones is totally contrary to the purity of abstraction. What was this shadowy element? It cannot be explained by the simple juxtaposition of mechanical and manual, rational and irrational, or man-made and natural. To my view, it was at the precise moment when he began his intercourse with the ocean that he became aware of the shadow, when he began to know the place or the material to which our bodies return. Perhaps for him the ocean might be like amniotic fluid, and therefore sinking into it would be like being absorbed back into the body itself, something which Plato excluded from his construction of pure form. About ten years after the *Purist Manifesto*, the body began to appear in Le Corbusier's paintings. This is not simply a change in subject. The body is expressed so vividly, and by careful observation it is combined with settings of seascapes and the spirals of shells from the sea.

Platonic pure form, or the world dominated by the transparent order of Phidias, also contains its opposite mythos: the world of darkness covered by an opaque cloud, the labyrinth of the Minotaur, for instance. Perhaps Minos was the one who constructed Crete, the first civilization of the Mediterranean. The ruler of the labyrinth, the Minotaur, was killed by the prince of Athens, Theseus, who was helped by the princess of Minos, Ariadne.

For Greeks, the labyrinth signified an opaque darkness. If the culture of Minos was on the island of Crete and the Labyrinth was the temple of Knossos, as is assumed today, the Greeks would probably have considered this domain to be as dark as the deepest depths of the ocean. The story of Ariadne might be

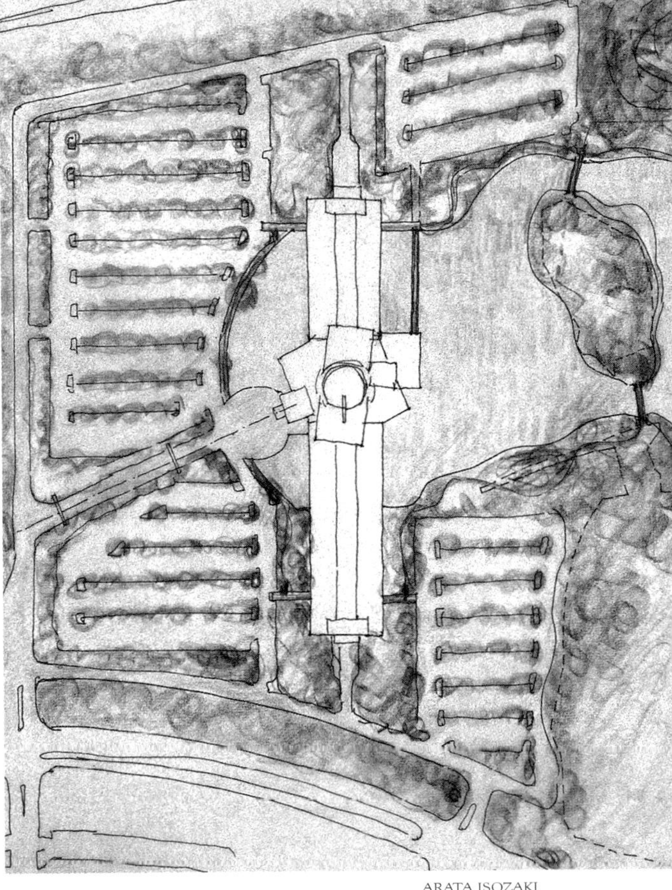

ARATA ISOZAKI

Rendering of the Team Disney building.

ARATA ISOZAKI

Isozaki's sketch of The Museum of Contemporary Art, Los Angeles, California.

suggesting that it is the sea itself that is considered to be the dark side of the spirit, something amorphic and uncanny.

I do not mean that Le Corbusier abandoned his purism entirely. Given that his purism is Platonic par excellence, as might be inferred from his writing, this turn marked the point at which his faith in clear logic began to be absorbed into the labyrinthine opacity. I have a strong feeling that the conversion was triggered by the Eros perceived only at the moment of sexual engorgement, namely, by the absolute substance that embraces the body as it expands and absorbs all physical activities.

It must have taken quite a long time until he finally became aware of the sense of directly descending into the darkness; this consciousness came to the fore rather gradually via the expression of the body in his paintings. He depicted the extremities of the human figure—head, hands, and genitalia—as metamorphosed and inflamed. These parts, which have the most complicated shapes of the body, are enlarged, made anonymous, and objectified. The head is twisted to the extent that it totally lacks features, except for eyes and lips. The vagina is deformed until it might be identified with some folk symbol.

Why did this rational man, who could have controlled everything within the logical frame and achieved transparency in painting, architecture, and writing, all of a sudden come to be involved in opaque objects? Why did he begin to use, or even overuse, the anti-industrial materials, stone and wood, that had long been abandoned?

I think that the conversion was motivated by his growing sense of the existence of the body that had begun to appear in his paintings. This is just conjecture without proof, and we cannot ask his body, now sunken and disseminated into the ocean. However, taking into consideration that the line of investigation that came to fruition in the Villa Savoye consciously omitted the shadow while it obstinately constructed the cubist drama, it might be possible to say that his coming to terms with the body motivated his conversion.

The existence of the body is the very uncontrollable sensation one experiences at the extremity of sexual engorgement, where all the controls of intellectual logic collapse and the visible world is instantaneously discharged into the infinitely expanding opaque material until it vanishes. By way of the sexual act, the body gives itself up to the uncontrollable expansion of darkness. Even if the mind once again manages to escape to the transparent world, the engorgement and expulsion recurs time and again to be ultimately connected to absolute darkness, the world of death. It should be said that Le Corbusier saw this wave of death that attacks incessantly. And once the darkness was uncovered, it quickly permeated his work. For instance, his discovery of *béton brut*, the raw texture of rough concrete, might be related to the landscape of a city deserted by war. But, rather, it seems to me that this use of *béton brut* was the achievement of his pursuit of the Eros of absurdity in materiality. If he had not seen the dark side, such materiality would have remained scorned and ignored. Because the potential of sexual engorgement dwells permanently in the body, he could not

JAQUELINE SALMON

Interior view of Le Corbusier's Convent Sainte-Marie de la Tourette.

Isozaki's Museum of Contemporary Art, Los Angeles, California, 1986.

have been totally detached from the corporeal, even in the time of purism. Yet it was at his departure from purism that he radically encountered the absurd body that engorges itself repeatedly. It is not only that he could not escape the darkness, but also that he dared to plunge into it. By elaborating the spiral space at the same time as pursuing the twisted genitalia, his pure figures became more opaque, and the raw and disordered materiality came to be more outstanding. Isn't it possible then that the result of his turn caused the worldwide permeation of the architecture of *béton brut* during the twenty years following the war?

I do not know yet if such an expression as "sexual space" is appropriate, but at least the Convent Saint-Marie de la Tourette is the place where I realized that a space could cause a sensation akin to sexual intercourse. The institution of the monastery was disbanded, and women are now allowed to enter the space, but it used to be a place for priests to practice asceticism, isolated in their own cells

THE MUSEUM OF CONTEMPORARY ART, LOS ANGELES, CALIFORNIA

and dedicating themselves to prayer and study.

A labyrinthine corridor goes around the living quarters that surround a courtyard. After being stimulated rhythmically by the daylight penetrating a sloping forest of concrete struts that is arranged according to the modulor, called *pan de verre rhythmique*, I descended into the darkness of a basement corridor where I could only grope. Then all of a sudden, when I came across a scene in which a brightly colored altar was illuminated by bundles of light shining through the cylindrical windows, *canon de lumière*, I was more than surprised; I was intoxicated by ecstasy.

This was nothing but a scene from the abyss. The daylight coming through the holes cut in various angles, some of its bands tainted with primary colors, being reflected on the interior cylinder. The visitors began to swim around the various objects constructed of the rough texture of *bêton brut* that are articulated by the brilliant and dimply glow. I thought that, facing the wall painted with red, yellow, and black, the monks must have had physical intercourse with the divinity.

There is no ground for the speculation that Le Corbusier had a conversion thirty years before the monastery was built. The only clue for the speculation was the darkness of the altar. After having produced various visual languages for thirty years, the opaque substance began to appear as a shadow of flesh congealed in the abyssal darkness deep in the monastery. Furthermore, although the plan is based upon the conventional style of the Dominican monastery, it unexpectedly produces spiral labyrinths all over by placing the living quarters in various spots around the courtyard. All the windows are systematically installed facing the surrounding forest, however, in the same sense as in the traditional monastery where the corridor surrounding the courtyard is one of the most important elements, and the gaze of visitors is planned to be oriented inward by the horizontally continuous windows, as well as by the modulor ones. And in the courtyard, there are so many geometric elements: cone, cylinder, cube, a sloped and welled triangular corridor, pillars with an irregular arch; together they form a rather chaotic ambiance.

THE MUSEUM OF CONTEMPORARY ART, LOS ANGELES, CALIFORNIA

Isozaki's Museum of Contemporary Art, Los Angeles, California, 1986.

In this, one cannot sense the same atmosphere as in his spaces of the 1920s of the so-called white period, in which transparent objects penetrate each other. In this courtyard, all objects, wildly exposed with no articulation, are allowed to collide with each other. What characterizes the labyrinthine aspect of this space is the opacity the architect called "the drama of light and shadow."

Le Corbusier never returned from his journey that began in Platonic transparent space and then radically shifted toward the labyrinthine space of the Minotaur. Isn't what we see at the Convent Saint-Marie de la Tourette the culmination of his journey? It is at least possible to say that all the forms he created are combined here; beginning with the modulor, and even including "the five principles of modern architecture," everything is fully applied, appearing and disappearing here and there. The texture of concrete is present at its roughest, used in such a way that no one could have applied it more roughly. Methodologically, this is a generalization of all the visual languages he pursued over his forty-year career. According to my belief, however, it was purely in order to express the unnamable space of ecstasy that all these languages were used. And in terms of his thematic, it was quite appropriate that it be a monastery for the Dominican order, a school of Catholicism in an anti-Hellenistic domain. Divinity cannot be reached sheerly by exposing the body; it is only possible to catch a glimpse of it at an instant—at the erotic moment attained by pushing the body into a corner where phantasmic illusion takes over. Prayer in the monastery is possible only by being fulfilled with such a subtle but intense eroticism. The internal space of the Convent Sainte-Marie de la Tourette makes me feel as if I were going down to the abyss, making a spiral dive into the Minotaur's labyrinth.

When I saw the snapshot, what came to mind was this: For Le Corbusier, dipping in the erotic space of ecstasy was equal to being embraced by the Mediterranean sea in his swimsuit. I have to admit that I am fascinated by the realm into which he dove: expelling the transparent order of Phidias, fumbling and deforming the vagina to make it into a skeletal relief, and staining a sticky shadow on the back of a coarse material, he finally constructed a space, in an abyssal darkness, in which to have intercourse with the divinity. In all of those moments the boundless ocean of the Mediterranean must have been swaying in his mind.

The ocean was ever present; it was permeating all of these events; it was because the ocean, namely Eros, was taking revenge on the distilled logic of transparency. Giving oneself to the ocean amounted to releasing all of one's muscles toward death, precisely as seen in the snapshot. It was symbolic that this architect, who persisted in struggling with the Other, chose the Mediterranean Ocean for his dênouement.

He died of a heart attack while he was drowning. The lesson is that the body cannot disperse itself into the ocean without going through such a practical procedure.

—*Translated by Sabu Kohso*

1 Plato, *Philebus*, translated by R. Hackforth, in *Plato: The Collected Dialogues*, edited by Edith Hamilton and Huntington Cairns, Bollington Series LXXI (Princeton University Press, 1961) 1132.

Carlos Jimenez

on

Luis Barragan

IN THE FALL OF 1978, during my third year in architecture school, I came across a catalogue from an architectural exhibition that was to have a great influence on my sensibilities. *The Architecture of Luis Barragan* had been held at the Museum of Modern Art in New York two years before, curated by the Argentine architect Emilio Ambazz. The exhibition

TIM STREET-PORTER

brought the work of the Mexican architect to the attention of a larger public for the first time since the 1950s. I was struck by the compelling image of the catalogue's cover: a mesmerizing still-life of walls and clouds suspended on a reflective black backdrop. This composition had an otherworldly effect, as if it had been extracted from an ancient yet familiar landscape. The image evoked the world of an artist who understood architecture to be the domain of the immeasurable, the elemental, the mysterious, its presence as necessary as water, bread, or light.

At the time of Barragan's exhibition, postmodernism was launching its revisionist movement in the world of architecture, propagating its role as antidote to the ills of modernism by producing instant, diluted historical facsimiles. Unable to relate to the movement's facile exploitation and appropriation of historical precedents, I found in the work of Barragan a luminous and inspiring alternative. I was impressed by the nakedness of the work, the utter simplicity of

TIM STREET-PORTER

PREVIOUS SPREAD: **Barragan's Capuchinas Sacramentarias del Purisimo Corazón de Maria, Tlalpan, Mexico, 1952–55.** ABOVE AND RIGHT: **Two interior views of the Gilardi House—the hallway with vertical windows *(right)* that leads to the dining room with pool *(above)*.**

TIM STREET-PORTER

each space unfolding its intense relationship with nature. Through this exchange, Barragan transcended stylistic concerns, as his work did not pretend to represent a particular school nor did it intend to fill the messianic call of another ideology. The work revealed the power of its emotive manifesto: a poetic interlude between the inevitability of space and the wonder of nature.

Some years later I was able to visit Barragan's works in Mexico City, and subsequently, a few of his earlier works in Guadalajara, where he was born in 1902. What I came to discover was the disparity between precious photographic images of the work (by now extensively disseminated in art and architecture circles) and the phenomenological effect that the works would generate when experienced in their respective context. Ironically, the architecture of Barragan, often celebrated through the fleeting incantation of the photographic image, is extremely difficult to capture through the camera's approximations. The best photographers of the architect's

PAUL HESTER

Exterior view of Jimenez Studio.

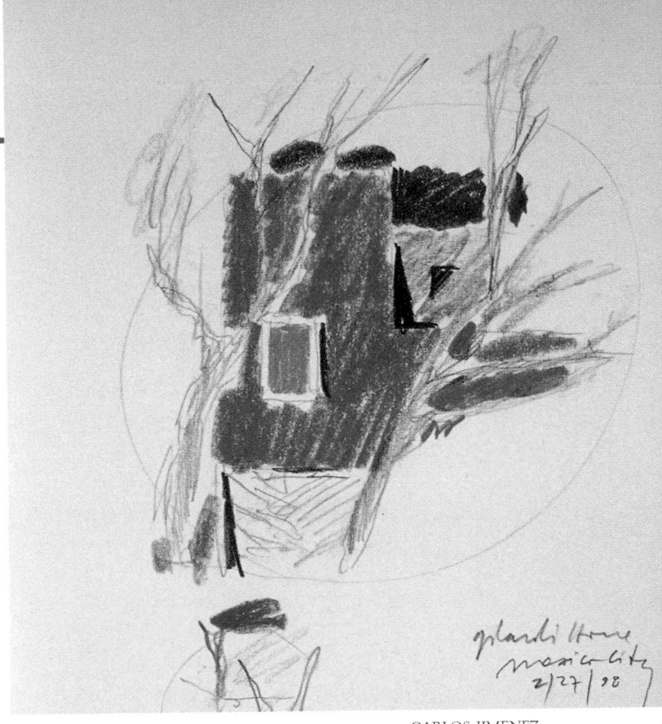

CARLOS JIMENEZ

CARLOS JIMENEZ

TOP: **Carlos Jiminez's sketch of the exterior of the Gilardi House.** ABOVE: **Detail of the completed structure.**

work have been able to suggest a common characteristic in it: the beauty of time experienced through the modest majesty of light. These photographers discharge the condensed power of the works, not as frozen images or exquisite compositions but as thresholds into the experience of the works. Throughout these images, one sees light as the ultimate material, which makes Barragan's fountains dazzle with their evanescent hues, and which conjures hidden domains from the most intense of colors.

Barragan wrote but a few reflections on his work, more like autobiographical epigrams. It is interesting that on reading them again I find a certain distrust for the dominance of the visual in his perception of the world. The eye for Barragan could at times be a deceptive sense, and one not always needed for seeing the nature of things. He trusted the power of all the senses in unison and in consonance with certain words that could evoke these sensual territories. One feels that words, for Barragan, were the first constructions of any architecture to be. Such words bridge the simultaneity or singularity of the senses with imagination. Thus, for Barragan, words like "magic," "garden," "serenity," and "surprise," to name a few, acquire an urgency in the construction of any

PAUL HESTER

PAUL HESTER

OPPOSITE: **Detail of Barragan's Capuchinas Sacramentarias del Purisimo Corazón de Maria.** ABOVE: **Jiminez's Lynn Goode Gallery, 1990.** RIGHT: **Exterior of secondary entry to Jiminez's Houston Museum of Fine Arts Administration and School Building, Texas, 1994.**

TIM STREET-PORTER

work. These words are not only the beginning of a work of architecture, but its ritual, its continuity, and its end. It is as if Barragan profoundly understood that all architectures are first bound by the landscapes that words evoke. The spaces of memory are not distant islands but ever-present seas. Poets know this, and Barragan, one of this century's most lucid poets, built with words that through water, light, and space manifest an irrepressible faith in the simple beauty of architecture.

CARLOS JIMENEZ

When thinking of Barragan, I am often reminded of the Mexican poet Octavio Paz's probing imagination as it searched among traditions in order to arrive at a more incisive and humanistic concept of modernity. It was Paz who wrote referring to Barragan's work that "To be truly modern we must first come to terms with our traditions." This is a modernity whose traces can be found in the inevitable reality of a singular place, the territory where memory and invention coexist. Barragan sought to invent, as exemplified by his best works, a way of living within the claustrophobic and saturated conditions of his adopted Mexico City, the world's most populated city. This invention is a living and personalized continuation of the architect's own spaces of memory, transformed by the enormous inspiration that a new place can exert on them. Thus the restorative gaze of gardens, the innumerable mirrors of water, or the millennial gestures of light, so impressed in Barragan's memory, inhabit the architect's works and their sites in total harmony.

Of all of Barragan's works that I have been able to visit, it is his own house (1947) and the convent and chapel for the Capuchin nuns (1955), both in Mexico City, which have impressed me the most. The physical and emotive spectrum that these two works release manifest the power of dwelling in the world—fully immersed in the spiritual edification that architecture slowly constructs. Located in the midst of highly dense and populated contexts, these

Carlos Jiminez's sketch of the interior of Barragan's house.

Interior view of the Houston Museum of Fine Arts Administration and School Building, Houston, Texas.

PAUL HESTER

works engulf one in an overwhelming feeling of serenity. As if in a prolonged pause, nature is discovered anew through the weight of its choreographed splendor. Thus a climbing tree or a wandering ivy, a corner of light or a blade of water, acquire an unbeknown gravity in the meaning of the architecture. This weighting is an invitation to dwell in things, to understand the marvel of their being. It is no wonder that for Barragan the totally glazed building was an anomaly of architecture, as he felt it offered no corner or niche from which to surprise or be surprised by nature.

I have collected these reflections on Barragan as evidence of the deep gratitude and admiration I feel for the work of this most humble of architects. Aristocratic in upbringing and manner yet deeply rooted in the splendid humility he found in the Catholic faith, Barragan sought to express this humility as the supreme obligation of the work of art. Intimate and universal, Barragan's work is like a mountain whose presence cannot be denied. It can be traversed back and forth across memory's arabesques or held captive amid the marvelous topography of two hands. Barragan's work ultimately reminds me of the great Russian filmmaker Andrei Tarkovsky's reflections on the creative act: "Perhaps the meaning of all human activity lies in artistic consciousness, in the pointless and selfless creative act? Perhaps our capacity to create is evidence that we ourselves were created in the image and likeness of God?"

Drawing from Le Corbusier's sketchbook of 1959.

Sumet Jumsai *on* Le Corbusier

The Open Hand

THE SKETCH BY LE CORBUSIER shows an event that took place in Cambridge in 1959 during my second year as an architectural student. L-C is shown in the middle of a procession of distinguished academics led by the vice chancellor of the university.

Clad in medieval scarlet robes and hats, they had just come out from the Senate House where L-C and Henry Moore had been earlier invested with honorary doctoral degrees.[1] Seen in a window above the procession is a student (myself) throwing confetti over the procession shouting L-C's own famous line "*A bas l'Academie!*" ("Down with universities!"). Actually, there were two more students from the School of Architecture in other windows, and perhaps the one in the drawing is supposed to represent all three of us. But since I was the most vociferous, L-C looked up at me.

SUMET JUMSAI

The *Open Hand* monument.

Years later in Bangkok, perhaps in the 1970s, William Curtis told me over a dinner about the drawing in L-C's sketchbooks that he was trying to identify for a publication. A brief description was enough for me to identify it for him.

Back in Cambridge, L-C invited me to go and stay with him in Chandigarh, which I did in 1964. When I turned up at the house, Pierre Jeanneret answered the door and, after complaining that L-C rarely came anymore and left him (Pierre) with all the problems, put me up in the master's bedroom.

It was an austere space, and the furnishing consisted of a "Van Gogh" chair, an Indian bed strung with cords and no mattress to speak of, and a forlorn dustbin. I was immensely impressed, as any architectural student of that generation would be. And the first thing I did was to scavenge the dustbin. There I found two crumpled sketches of the *Open Hand*. But to this day I cannot find them, having put them away so very carefully between the pages of one of the numerous books in my library.

Earlier this year I went again to Chandigarh, this time to participate in the conference "Celebrating Chandigarh—50 Years of the Idea."[2] The *RIBA*

Journal a fortnight before the event, labeled it as a get-together of the old fogeys and called L-C an imposter (which is rather surprising coming from the RIBA). But then, of course, it was the old fogey's last tango. However, the majority at the conference were the younger people and architectural students, and, as in the 1950s and the 1960s, the air was charged with the freshness of inspiration and innocent expectation that can rarely be experienced nowadays.

The conference inauguration took place in the pit at the *Open Hand* monument. As speakers took to the lectern, the audience huddled together under a cold breeze while the metal-clad *Hand* pivoted on a column, with ballbearings gently turning in the wind like a weathercock.

My mind drifted from the pit to the Governor's Palace, which Charles Correa had made out of white cloth covering over a specially erected scaffolding to silhouette against the Himalayan foothills—a reminder for the Indian government to complete L-C's scheme for the Capitol—and away from the foothills to the outlines of the Assembly and the Secretariat in the distant haze.

As the *Hand* turned with a cranky metallic sound, my thoughts shifted to Stanley Kubrick's *2001—A Space Odyssey*. I saw humanoids in the opening scene fingering the Tablet, trying to understand it, followed by a tribal fight with one group grabbing bones and sticks to beat up the other. The message was that the beginning of tooling or tooling extension of the limbs had begun, or what archaeologists call "industry." The big jump, in the next scene, was the intelligent spaceship: the ultimate tooling extension of humans at the start of the third millennium. The hand and its tooling extension have become man's link to the cosmos.

But the hand is also the means to communicate amongst earthlings, whether before or after the written language was formulated. In the Hindu-Buddhist world the hand language is all pervasive; for example, the Buddha's statue with open hands in the frontal position signifies peace and amelioration as well as the shunning of temptation. Then there are the classical dances using the hand language—Indian, Thai, Cambodian, Balinese, etc.

The Thai *svasti* or Indian *namasti* is another prevalent hand posture when paying respect to fellow humans or when praying as also adopted by Christians. The hand language is endless, and it applies to all people including the deft and dumb, palmists and protesters in the streets.

For more than four years, L-C made some 200 sketches of the *Open Hand*, several models and a full-size mock-up for the eventual monument. He made impassioned pleas to Nehru, his client and patron, to have the *Hand* built as the crowning symbol of Chandigarh. Fate has it that it was built only in 1986, or twenty-one years after he died.

There are already a number of essays on L-C's hand symbolism.[3] I will now write down all the inferences associated with it:

- A gesture to heaven or cosmos—possibly an offering.
- To receive and to give ("*Pleine main j'ai reçu. Pleine main je donne*," L-C's poem of 1959).
- Peace and reconciliation. Picasso's *Dove of Peace*

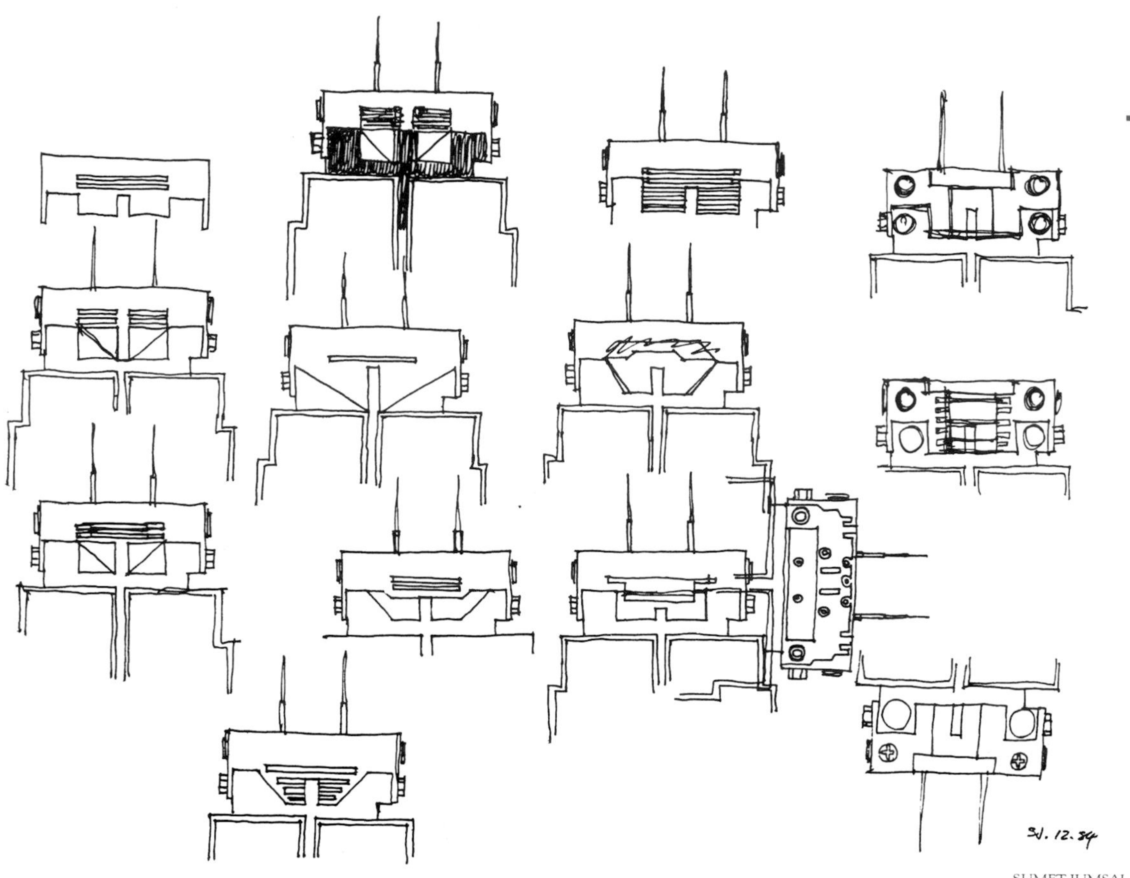

SUMET JUMSAI

Jumsai's sketches of the Robot Building, 1984.

comes to mind in this instance. The hand's profile, in fact, is birdlike.

- Hand as a human tool, leading to tooling extension, i. e., machines, "the instruments of progress and civilization." The latter quote was the principal credo of both L-C and Nehru in connection with the new planning and modern architecture at Chandigarh. The city was to kick-start the dormant civilization onto the road of modernization. This was the way both client and architect thought India could be revitalized and become once more a leading civilization in the modern world.
- Opening up to the element, the open air and all that it implies: freedom, health, Esprit Nouveau, the spirit of the Renaissance man, etc.
- Freedom which in turn equals work, and vice versa, in that work can be equated to freedom.[4]
- Actually, the aspect concerning the offering at the foot of the Himalayas shows L-C being innocent of Hindu cosmology. I don't think he knew that the Himalayas was Mount Meru, pivot of the universe. To come to terms with it, a mere gesture of the hand was insufficient. Harmony with the cosmos in the Hindu/Buddhist concept means replication of the cosmology in city planning and architecture.[5]
- L-C's *Hand* at the foot of Mount Meru was evidently in the European tradition: humanistic, anthropomorphic, and sculptural. Moreover, the em-

phasis on the hand goes back to the artist-sculptor's instinct, and we also see similar manifestations in Michelangelo, Ozenfant, Léger, and Picasso. In effect, with the sculptor, all the limbs tend to be emphasized and exaggerated: muscular arms and legs and big feet. That the hand receives more attention is due to the fact that a host of possibilities are here: mystical, sublime, or purely sculptural on a personal and abstract level. L-C's paintings since the 1930s exhibited this sculptor's penchant for oversized limbs, and the hand as his leitmotif began from that period.

Plasticity runs through L-C's work together with another great European tradition: the use of ideal geometry and proportions, including those of the human body. Ronchamp, Sainte-Marie de la Tourette, and Chandigarh, designed at about the same time, show L-C at the height of his sculptural period. (Ronchamp is, of course, the most poetic.) In the meanwhile, proportions permeate from the early villas to the application of the Modulor in the design of the *Open Hand*.

I suppose my works reverberate after L-C's sculptural period of the 1950s. But looking back it was more than a love affair with plasticity. Somehow the anthropomorphic side of L-C's symbolism—the hand—also came into play. Together with the early cubism of Braque, Picasso, L-C, and Chirico—and I am thinking, for example, of Picasso's *Harlequin* of 1915 and Chirico's composition of the same period—I began to see a new grammar emerging in my own work.

In the accompanying illustration of the poster I used at the Venice Biennale 96 (page 96), three projects are shown.[6] At the top is the Robot Building of

PROFILE

Robot Building, head office of Bank of Asia, Bangkok, 1986.

1986 (Bank of Asia head office in Bangkok). It is quite a literal statement in robotic design, although the underlying philosophy is exorcism of the machine. The middle picture, the Nation Building of 1991 (head office of *The Nation Newspaper*) represents a metamorphosis of the Robot. In this case it is a cutout or profile of the chief editor sitting and working on his word processor. He is infused with electronic circuitry, and from this vantage point other elevations or cutouts are already discerned with more electronic imagery but with receding anthropomorphic associations, so that on the other side of the "building" the editor's profile becomes merely an abstract shape dominated by computer chips and circuits.

SJA+3D

Poster at the Venice Biennale, 1996.

The bottom pictures in the poster show the design in 1995–97 for a UN-related institute at the Place des Nations, Geneva. (Five architects—Fuksas, Eisenman, myself, Koolhaas, and Perrault—were each assigned to design one building in this new UN complex, but the people of Geneva scrapped the entire project in a referendum in 1998.) The one on the right, an earlier competition version, is a straightforward reinterpretation of cubism, and on the left a sketch that led to the final design. The latter is a continuation of the Nation Building and it also results in the 1998 design proposal for MOCAB (Museum of Contemporary Art–Bangkok). Here, cubism is simplified to the utmost, while the whole is a sculpture, a public art.

I have been told that my work is iconic, i.e., noncontextual and hermetic, a finished product and not a process. If that is the case, then I am a confirmed Corbusian, for L-C's architecture is iconic. All this is possibly blasphemous to the present generation, who like Vishnu, who destroys in order to create, must deconstruct in order to reassemble in a continuous process—all of which is admittedly healthy. But a little sense of history, or irony, will tell anyone that the most violent deconstruction occurred in Cubism.

So there we were, in the pit under the revolving *Open Hand*, fogeys and non-fogeys, none of who have managed to escape from L-C.

Nation Building, head office of *The Nation Newspaper*, east side, Bangkok, 1991.

A. KAMPRASERT

1 The idea of L-C receiving a doctorate at Cambridge came from Colin Rowe, who was teaching there.

2 The conference was initiated by Charles Correa. It took place 8–11 January 1999.

3 *The Open Hand, Essays on Le Corbusier*, edited by Russell Walden (MIT Press, 1977).

4 This point might be stretched to link with Ruskin's or the Pre-Raphaelite's idea of honest (manual) work associated with English paternalism.

5 Cf. *Naga*, Sumet Jumsai (Oxford University Press, 1988).

6 The logo for the Biennale was actually the hand, and we all had to send in photographs of our hands for the catalogue. A giant hand sculpture was also erected on the canal side near the exhibition venue.

Villagrán's Parking Garage, Mexico City, 1948.

INSTITUTO NACIONAL DE BELLAS ARTES

Ricardo Legorreta *on* José Villagrán

IN 1951, I WAS STUDYING at the Universidad Nacional Autónoma de México, which was founded in 1553, the oldest university in North America. The different schools were spread throughout the historic center of Mexico City, with the Architectural School being one of the most outstanding. At that time, there was a strong movement at the school to create con-

INSTITUTO NACIONAL DE BELLAS ARTES

Villagrán's access ramp to the Mundet Maternity Clinic, Mexico City, 1952

temporary architecture under the leadership of the former dean and distinguished theory professor, José Villagrán.

The Architecture School was located in the heart of the historic center of Mexico City, two blocks from the main square, and occupying the Academia de San Carlos, a fine building built in 1783. Because the different schools were spread throughout the city and most of the teachers were practitioners, classes were either very early or very late at night. This gave me the opportunity to study and to enjoy the buildings and lifestyle of the old city during the day.

In one of my walks, I noticed a building under construction that was in the final stages of finishing details. Mesmerized, I studied the building for hours—starting with the window details and finishing with a four-hour walk-through tour. I was astonished by the architect's understanding of urban scale, the relation of structure to architecture, the use of natural light and ventilation, and maintenance considerations—all of which were solved in a contemporary way that integrated the scale of the city's historic center. At this time, none of these concepts were important to most of our teachers. When the tour finished, I asked who the architect was and learned that it was my architectural theory teacher,

José Villagrán. He had designed this building that I had so admired! I decided then and there that I wanted to work for him.

José Villagrán was the most respected architect in the country and the philosophical leader, playing a role similar to Walter Gropius in the Bauhaus. Like Gropius, perhaps his greatest impact was in the area of architectural education.

Villagrán was born in Mexico, raised and educated by Jesuits, and later studied at the Universidad Nacional Autónoma de México. When he was

INSTITUTO NACIONAL DE BELLAS ARTES

Villagrán's Hospital de Jesús, Mexico City, 1943.

INSTITUTO NACIONAL DE BELLAS ARTES

Mundet Sports Park, Mexico City, 1943.

LOURDES LEGORRETA

Legorreta's College of Santa Fe Visual Arts, New Mexico, 1999.

twenty-eight years old, he was appointed dean of the School of Architecture and remained as a teacher until his death in 1982.

The modern movement in Mexico was firmly rooted in and propelled by the ideals of the revolution, a movement that affected both the practice and teaching of architecture.

José Villagrán had tremendous influence in the field of medical building design. In the years around 1925, he was the chief architect for the Department of Public Health, and he was able to produce and build a number of medical facilities.

In the 1920s, Villagrán taught architectural theory at the conservative school of the Academy of San Carlos, the only school in the country that offered an architectural program. Later, he was appointed Director of the New Faculty of Architecture at the Universidad Nacional Autónoma de México (UNAM), which had broken away from San Carlos. Villagrán went on to design a good part of the UNAM's main campus, including the architecture school, and finally became a member of its Board of Regents.

During his lifetime, he designed numerous buildings, from hospitals, markets, and offices to private houses. He also wrote several books and was highly recognized in Mexico, as well as abroad.

A highly cultured man, Villagrán devoted his life to creating architecture that was socially and economically suited to his country, and all without the excesses in design and cost. He was the first to teach the tenets of modernism, even though he was a professor of architectural theory.

I applied for a job with Villagrán's firm and was accepted as a draftsman. When I told my father about my new job, he told me that he was a former classmate of Villagrán's. I asked my father not to tell Villagrán about me. After six months of working in the drafting room, Villagrán finally noticed me. When he learned that I was the son of Luis Legorreta, he was impressed that I did not use my father's name to get the job.

For fourteen years I worked for Villagrán—from draftsman to associate. During those years, I learned a side of architecture that is normally disregarded. I learned that architecture is a social service, that a building should respond to a program and a budget, and that good construction is essential. Villagrán made me fall in love with architecture. At his side, I

Legorreta's Metropolitan Cathedral in Managua, Nicaragua, 1994.

LOURDES LEGORRETA

LOURDES LEGORRETA

Legorreta's Solana Complex Westlake-Southlake, Dallas, Texas, 1990.

learned that architecture was not only the most beautiful profession in the world but that it was a profession where not only the aesthetics are important but also a strong social consciousness is required.

I realized as an architect that I had an important role to play in solving the needs of the masses. I thought, "First we will make houses for the people. Esthetes and rhetoricians can have their debates later." By working long days and weekends, I learned that the design process is endless and that we are primarily builders—we cannot design something if we do not know how to build it.

Once while visiting a construction site, Villagrán pointed out to a worker that the brick wall was poorly executed. He received the usual answer: "The brick is not good as it used to be." Villagrán called the foreman and got the same answer. Then, he, the master of architecture, who was always dressed in a conservative and impeccable way, took his jacket and tie off, rolled up his sleeves, asked the worker for his tools, and built thirty square feet of perfect wall. Everyone was astonished. He then turned to me and said, "Remember, Ricardo, above everything we are builders."

I was fortunate enough to be present during his frequent and deep discussions with structural and mechanical engineers about how good architecture is always in harmony with engineering. Many times I saw José Villagrán, with great patience and courtesy, "educating" a client in what architecture is and what architecture is not.

He taught us to understand the complexity of Mexican culture and encouraged us to design with a social consciousness—to fight against the merchants of construction and to stand firmly in front of "uncultured" clients. I learned from him that the architect must maintain his dignity and to stand up for his beliefs in front of all, whether it is his client or his contractor.

Even though I did not agree with many of Villagrán's design theories, I am immensely grateful to him for leaving me with the conviction that architects should design for the users and not for an ego or for the architectural elite. One of the most valuable experiences in my life has been the opportunity of meeting and working with José Villagrán.

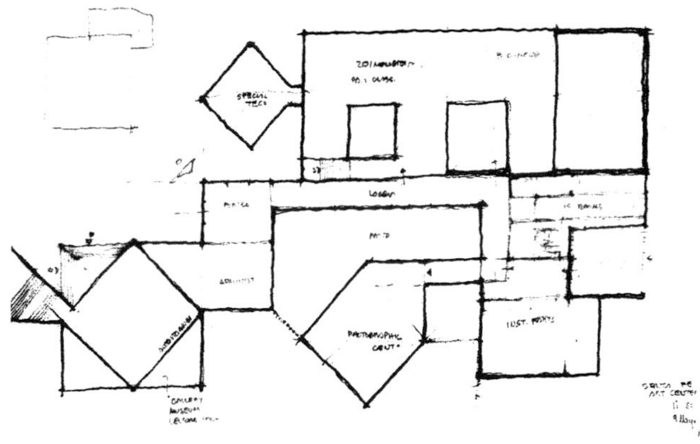

RICARDO LEGORRETA

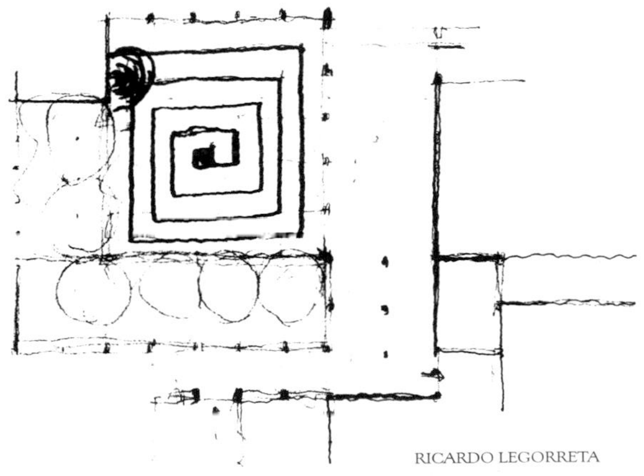

RICARDO LEGORRETA

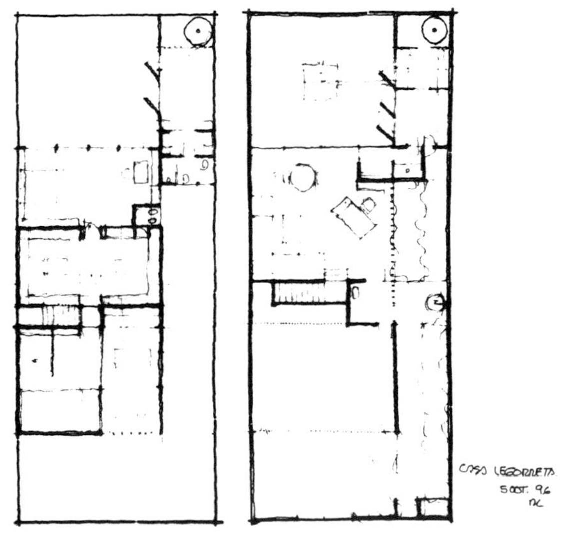

RICARDO LEGORRETA

TOP AND CENTER: **Sketches of the Visual Arts Building, College of Santa Fe, Santa Fe, New Mexico.**
RIGHT: **Casa Legorreta.**

William S. W. Lim

on

Le Corbusier

From Corb to Gehry

Born in Hong Kong, trained in London, and a practice in Singapore, the influences on my professional career are both local and global as well as from multidisciplinary sources. My design approach and philosophy are multifaceted and are continuously evolving. They are based on existentialist-inspired pluralism, freedom, and tolerance and eastern holistic irrationality as well as the all-embracing goals of equity and social justice. To identify the influences of architects on my professional career is therefore not a simple task.

After finishing first-year architecture in Hong Kong University, I arrived in London in 1951 to join the Architectural Association, School of Architecture. At nineteen years

LUCIEN CLERGUE

LUCIEN CLERGUE

PREVIOUS SPREAD: **Detail of Le Corbusier's Palais de L'Assembleé, Capitol Buildings, Chandigarh, India, 1962.** ABOVE: **Le Corbusier's Secretariat, Capitol Buildings, Chandigarh, India, 1958.**

old, I was naturally impressionable and very eager to learn. I was intellectually and culturally shocked and suffered from information overload.

During my past two years at the AA, I was fortunate to be "adopted" by John Killick—a brilliant teacher. Through him, I got to know Bill Howell, James Stirling, and Peter and Alison Smithson. Killick's near obsession with Le Corbusier was both an inspiration and eye-opener to me, like wearing blinkers and having blind spots. In 1954, my housing project—inspired by Unité d'Habitation and Roehampton and using the complex ratios and measurements of the Modular—won me a travel grant to Europe. I visited most of Corb's buildings and was surprised by the noncompliance to the rules of modernism of the nearly completed Maison Jaoul and the incredibly inspiring Chapel at Ronchamp. I read all of his books available in English. I attended the Congres Internationaux d'Architecture Moderne (CIAM) meeting in Marseille and witnessed Corb's obvious delight at the successful maneuvering in its drastic transformation, i.e. the dissolution of CIAM and the formation of Team 10, comprising progressive young architects from different countries. In short, on completing my course at the AA, I had understood fully the Modern Movement, but mainly through Corb's perspective.

My stay at Harvard in 1956–57 gave me a broader insight into the historical development of the Modern Movement, including the fascinating Bauhaus experiments. I was also exposed to the current intellectual debate on existentialism, particularly of Sartre and Camus. However, like my contemporaries in the UK, Corb was still the greatest and symbolized modernism itself.

Living in Paris during turbulent interwar years, it appeared impossible for Corb to insulate himself from the intellectual discourse of existentialism and other radical alternatives. This was enforced by Kenneth Frampton's statement: "It is my contention that after 1930, Le Corbusier no longer believed in the Purist project as the manifest destiny of the machine-age civilization"[1] and by implication the assumed dominance and cultural superiority of Western technological civilization.

In the early 1960s, I visited Chandigarh, India. I was completely surprised by the intensive use of the Parasal—an overhanging roof protecting the spaces beneath from sun and rain—and the *brise-soleil*—the vertical sun-breakers. Corb's genius was his ability to generate symbolic forms that were right for the climate and appropriate for the crude technology available, as well as responsive to local culture and tradition. To quote William Curtis: "[Corb's] Indian works touched ancient memories within the traditions of the subcontinent...and were able to express the democratic ideas of a newly independent country."[2] Indeed, the fiftieth-year celebration of Chandigarh in January 1999 was an important occasion to generate serious discourse on the meaning of and lessons from projects of Corb and their impact on the subsequent development of architectural thoughts.

In 1960, together with two other returned graduates—we started a practice called Malayan Architects Co-Partnership. Some years later, there were problems of divergences in design approach as

WILLIAM LIM ASSOCIATES

Section of Lim's Golden Mile Complex, Singapore, 1974.

WILLIAM LIM ASSOCIATES

Lim's Central Square, Kuala Lumpur, Malasia, 1990.

well as incompatibility of personalities. It was only after Design Partnership was formed in 1967, that many major projects with clearly Corb-inspired design were constructed. They included Singapore Telephone Board Exchange (1969), People's Park Complex (1973), and Golden Mile Complex (1974). These projects made serious efforts to interpret, adopt, modify, and reinvent the spirit of Corb's ideas. They needed to be cost-effective, technologically appropriate, and climatically responsive in a rapidly changing physical, social, and political environment. These special conditions had generated new challenges and opportunities. For example, People's Park Complex is a large multistoried urban shopping center under one roof with its two interlocking atriums. The main atrium, which we called the City Room, was inspired by the ideas of the Metabolist Group

SCOTT GILCHRIST ARCHIVISION

Frank O. Gehry's house, Santa Monica, California. Date: ongoing.

in Japan. When Fumihiko Maki visited the building during its construction, he said, "We theorized and you people are getting it built."

Since the 1960s, I continued to intensify my involvement with intellectuals in the region. The oil crisis in the early 1970s, together with the adverse response from Singapore authorities on our critical comments, had resulted in a serious setback for the practice, and consequently the need to restructure the firm.

This period of enforced slowdown coincided with the new architectural development of postmodernism in the U.S. and elsewhere. I visited Tokyo and was particularly struck by the experiments of the post-Metabolist work of young Japanese architects. I became convinced that modern architecture, particularly the corporate version generally referred to as International Style, was neither understood nor appreciated by the common people whom it claimed to serve. It was in this context that I began to critically examine the Post-Modern Movement. I readily accepted their attack on modernism more than their varied solutions as shown in their works and writings. For the next few years, I concentrated my energy on trying out small- and medium-sized experimental projects—working closely with younger architects in the practice. Meanwhile, conflicts with my ex-partners increased. Eventually, I decided at the age of forty-nine to start a new practice under the name of William Lim Associates.

In 1982, I met up with Frank Gehry for the first time since our Harvard days. We renewed our student friendship. Together with my younger partner Mok Wei Wei, we visited his office, his home, and his other works in Los Angeles. Gehry and I spent a lot of time just talking. We met again on several occasions. What excited me about Gehry was his enthusiasm and commitment. Like a true artist, he is totally absorbed in the process of creativity as an end in itself.

No doubt Gehry has a strong influence on some projects in our practice. They include: Central Square, Kuala Lumpur (1990); Pasir Ris South Community Club, Singapore (1988 and 1992); Gallery Evason Hotel, Singapore (2000); and the Marine Parade Community Club, Singapore (2000).

Living in California in the midst of the existentialist-inspired value and cultural revolution, the rebellious spirit is in the air everywhere. Pop culture, drug culture, Eastern mysticism, and lifestyle experiments were there altogether. For the rebellious and the creative, California is fertile ground indeed. Bob Dylan composed folk songs and poems like *Times They are a Changin'*. James Dean rebelled without a cause. And Gehry?

Gehry designed cardboard furniture, his fish and his house and later the binocular building on Main Street in Venice. These products went far be-

TEH JOO-HENG

Lim's Gallery Evason Hotel, Singapore, 2000. Juxtaposition of various architectural elements.

yond conventional responses or current aesthetic criteria. Unlike the East Coast intellectual postmodernists, Gehry is a one-man band and a spiritual crusader. In his house, he changed the aesthetic norm by blurring boundaries between beauty and ugliness and by deregulating fragmentation. Together with his use of contrasting materials and their seemingly random spatial composition, his work can be described as a creative Western response to what I call Asian "holistic irrationality."

In the last decade, Gehry has produced numerous masterpieces including his incredible Guggenheim Museum at Bilbao, Spain. However, in my opinion, none can match the raw creative energy and unrestrained rebelliousness of his earlier statements.

In a world of rapid value and technological changes, architecture is ever changing, multidirectional, investigative, and unrestrained. However, this is not anarchy. It is unity in diversity and acceptance of the reality in the age of uncertainty. The present multidirectional development in urbanism, architecture, and the arts reflects the spirit of creative freedom and rebelliousness. Increasingly, pluralism is becoming the accepted norm. The criteria for excellence are being modified, developed, and expanded continuously. There is now no single standard solution which can be applied effectively. We should have no hang-up about *isms*—be they modern, late modern or post-

OPPOSITE: **View of a partially shaded basketball court, Marine Parade Community Club, Singapore, 2000.**

TAN KAH-HENG

TAN KAH-HENG

ABOVE: **Lim's Marine Parade Community Club, junction between Community Club and Marine Parade Regional Library, Singapore, 2000.** BELOW: **Frank O. Gehry's Disney Ice Rink, Anaheim, California.**

TIMOTHY HURSLEY

modern. It is in this context of the de-styling of architecture that I have credited the importance of Corb and Gehry in my own professional development.

1 Kenneth Frampton, "The Other Le Corbusier: Primitive Form and the Linear City," 1929–52, in *Le Corbuser: Architect of the Century* (Great Britain: Balding and Mansell UK Limited, 1987) 29.

2 William Curtis, "Le Corbusier: Nature and Tradition" in *Le Corbusier: Architect of the Century* (Great Britain: Balding and Mansell UK Limited, 1987) 21–22.

CHICAGO HISTORICAL SOCIETY, BILL HEDRICH, HEDRICH–BLESSING HB-04414-D3

Richard Meier

on

Frank Lloyd Wright

When Frank Lloyd Wright died in 1959, I was just two years removed from graduation from Cornell University, but it was not until four years later, after I had begun working on my own as an architect, that I had the opportunity to visit Fallingwater, the Edgar and Lillian Kaufmann house located deep in the woods, on Bear Run, a mountain stream in southwestern Pennsylvania.

I had, of course, seen many photographs of the Kaufmann house at Fallingwater and thought that I knew it from the drawings that I had seen; but what most impressed me on seeing it firsthand was the extraordinary siting in which the house was laid out at a sixty-degree angle to the entrance roadway and the waterfall, cantilevered dramatically over the rocks and the water. The view of the house from the entry road was on a diagonal similar to the way in which one sees it from the flat rock boulders in the stream below.

To me, Fallingwater was most beautifully conceived in its integration with the landscape and the way in which the underlying order of the design, the parallel walls and piers, which seem to grow out of the rock ledge on the north shore of the stream, support the mass of the house hovering above.

Fallingwater, designed in 1935, was much smaller than I thought it would be. Its scale was very intimate. The complex-spatial order, the horizontal, vertical, and diagonal relationships of interlocking spaces leading from one to another, from the interior to the exterior, was infused with opposition, tension, drama, and cohesion. Wright had created a very complex interior and exterior circulation system—overflowing horizontally with stairways, balconies, trellises, bridges, terraces, walks, passageways, and drives extending and overlapping through space—the cascading waterfall was only one part of his complex conceptual continuum motif. The horizontal thrusts interpenetrate one another and in many different planes shift and turn and twist in a manner that is analogous to the movement of the watercourse as it descends over the rocks below.

PREVIOUS SPREAD: **Fallingwater, Edgar J. Kaufmann house, Bear Run, Pennsylvania, 1939.**

The overall configuration of the plan of Fallingwater has a fractured stepping system of walls, piers, and volumes that respond to the contour lines of the diagonal rock ledge on which it sits. The counterbalancing of forces, horizontal and vertical, linear and stepping, symmetrical and casual, are planned in order to define a hierarchy of spaces and to stabilize the composition both on the interior and the exterior. The main living room is almost symmetrical. It is anchored by the stone fireplace that grows from the natural rock outcroppings in the watercourse below. The most symmetrical portion of this space is on the front, the waterside, and there is a more casual arrangement on the rear, the entry, and the sides. The fireplace is located on one side opposite the entry, and the water stair is positioned opposite from the study. The living space is defined by a slightly raised ceiling with lighting at its center. Intimate alcoves for sitting, dining, and study surround this great central space. The main living space, animated by natural light, reveals the whole and connects to that which is above, below, and beyond.

The entry, kitchen, stairs, and bedrooms are also asymmetrically arranged, in response to the diagonal northern rock ledge of the hill in the rear. This plan arrangement appears to be informal and responsive to the nature of the terrain; however, the overall effect is a masterpiece of organization that results in a very carefully disciplined order.

Wright was interested in the whole movement system—the circulation path of how you go from one place to another—the sequences of space, the interior spaces feeling man-made enclosed by natural stone, vertical walls in relation to open, light-colored, hori-

CHICAGO HISTORICAL SOCIETY, BILL HEDRICH, HEDRICH-BLESSING HB-04414-G3

Living room at Fallingwater.

zontal, reinforced concrete terraces reaching out to the landscape and gorge.

There is a dynamic relationship between the house and the land, between the flowing water and its solid foundations, between interior and exterior, between man-made and nature, between vertical and horizontal, and between mass and floating. The house embodies Wright's powerful teaching that it is in the nature of any organic building to grow from its site. Only by being there, seeing it, and experiencing the uniqueness of this magnificent place does one fully understand the way the building heightens our awareness of the site, bringing it to life in new ways.

In addition to Wright's intention to bring the outside into the house, there is in Wright's planning the continuity of geometric ordering—how one element is related to another—the creation of enclosure and openness, opacity and transparency, tension and movement, all of which come together in this extraordinary dwelling. Wright's carefully composed articulation of structure and circulation—with his system of opposites and contradictions—generated a forceful piece of architecture that has a simple meditative quality about it.

My architecture does not look like Wright's architecture, and while some of Le Corbusier's architecture might seem to be a more obvious pictorial reference, it is through my interpretation of Wright's

© SCOTT FRANCES/ESTO

© SCOTT FRANCES/ESTO

TOP: **Exterior of Meier's Grotta residence, Harding Township, New Jersey, 1985–89.**
ABOVE: **View from the interior of the Grotta residence.**

principles that certain precepts of his are discernible in my work.

I do not think about Wright, nor do I think about his buildings, when I am doing my own work. But I do think about certain architectural ideas—say, how to express a transparent open space, as opposed to a closed opaque one. Wright of course did it one way, and I do it another. In my opinion, Wright was wrong in some of the things that he said. But I find that interesting. You can learn as much from the oppositions as you can from the strengths. In believing Wright, I have learned to disbelieve Wright.

My architecture utilizes geometry and light to create a perpetual flow of circulation and continuity between the building and the landscape. Certain forms provide movement—not necessarily alone by themselves, but placed against their opposites they create a high level of conscious or unconscious energy. Often the simplest forms have the highest energy. Different forms may move at different speeds—long ramp against a short plane, for example, or a complex spiraling staircase juxtaposed against a flat white plane.

When I was in high school I read Frank Lloyd Wright's autobiography and Henry Russell Hitchcock's *In the Nature of Materials*; but it was not until my second year at Cornell University that I actually had a chance to meet Frank Lloyd Wright and to hear him lecture. He was very impressive, and during his week-long visit to Cornell, all of the architectural students would follow him around campus, and he would wave his cape and talk about his work with the students.

He was notorious for not admitting that he was

© SCOTT FRANCES/ESTO

Exterior of the Grotta residence.

influenced by anything but by nature—and if he thought he could have gotten away with it, he would have said that even there, he was the true originator. Everything and everyone else only "confirmed his thoughts." Wright felt that he was omnipotent.

Wright thought architecture was organic, and he believed that there is such a thing as natural materials. But a house cannot grow out of its site. Once you cut down a tree it is no longer organic; it is inorganic.

Architecture is not the product of a natural process. Buildings are made up of materials that in a strict sense cease to live—that no longer grow. They are unearthed and are no longer part of a fluctuating and metamorphic cycle—the architect is therefore engaged in an act of willful artificiality.

It has been my intention to propose an alternate form of integration that is pursued through a very intentional process of dematerialization. This has to do with an attempt to subvert the specific character

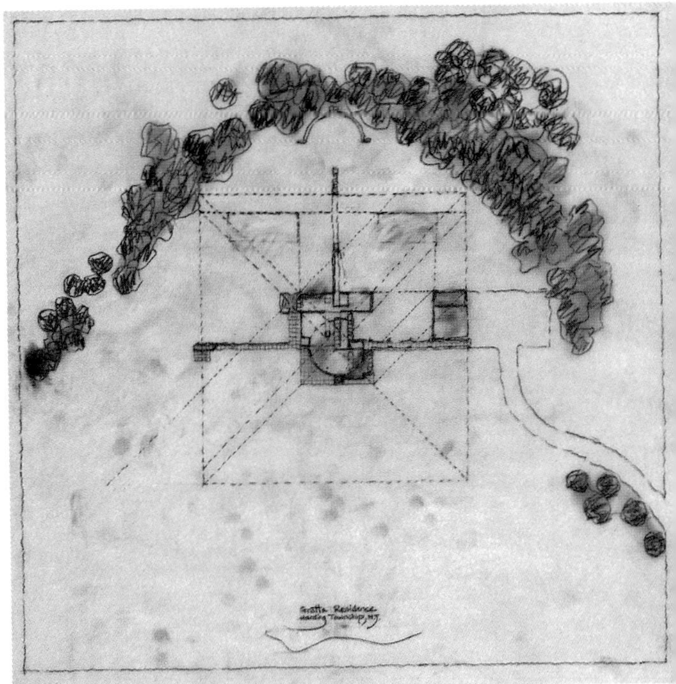

© RICHARD MEIER

Meier's sketch of the Grotta residence.

of the architectural surface itself in favor of the character of light and shadow, of context and occupant, that plays against it. One might think of this as a process aimed at materializing the matter of the frame so that the character of the framed is that much more intense. I am committed to a rigorous investigation of the physical consequences of such an operation.

Wright assiduously avoided using white; he preferred the life-giving color of a blood red. He had said that white is not of this earth. Yet seeing colors is a matter of what one has experienced or what one has been taught. What one thought was white yesterday may not be white tomorrow. One has only to look. One has only to be receptive. White is a reflective opaque surface that heightens the details placed against it—often the details are of nature itself. Nature presents white so we may see her colors. White also creates an ambiguous space—it reads as a flat surface and as an infinite void. Together, geometric forms and light have the power to grant the unexpected. The interpretation lies between the creator and the viewer. Perhaps different in program, perhaps different in form, but the presence and force exist.

Wright used light as if it were "a natural building material." His intercourse of light and shade was an artistic expression of his concept of continuity. Certainly he thought in terms of light for his private spaces (the bedrooms), which are fairly dark—very small, almost cell-like—unlike the living spaces, which flowed out onto the terraces, into the passageways, staircases, and balconies.

I utilize geometry in light to create a spirit of place. People who have lived in or visited my houses have spoken of an "experience." This experience, whether it lasts a few moments or has had a lasting profound impression, is what every architect hopes to achieve.

As T. S. Eliot said, "Genuine poetry can communicate before it is understood."[1]

Essay based on an interview with the editor, Susan Gray.

1 T. S. Eliot (Faber and Faber).

© SCOTT FRANCES/ESTO

ABOVE: **Exterior of the Grotta residence.** OPPOSITE: **View from its interior.**

© SCOTT FRANCES/ESTO

View of roof garden of Rockefeller Center's British Empire Building and lower plaza ice-skating rink.

MICHAEL MORAN

William Pedersen *on* Rockefeller Center

ARCHITECTURE THAT PLACES fundamentally opposing ideas into conflict and brings about an artistic equilibrium from their opposition is my greatest source of inspiration. Within a single work of architecture, conflict can be sponsored by a variety of issues. Its resolution requires the controlling hand of a central idea that weaves the opposing strands into a whole that is stronger than the aggregate of its parts. Conceived during great prosperity, designed and executed during a period of economic

MICHAEL MORAN

despair, Rockefeller Center, carefully examined, reveals in both its architecture and its process of design numerous paradoxes whose resolution has brought about the greatest urban architectural assemblage of the twentieth century. The architecture that we revere today is the result of what must have been a titanic effort; a contemporary equivalent of the labors of Hercules as he passed through the crucible of agony on his arduous journey to attain the status of a god. One can extrapolate this parallel from the statue at Rockefeller Center of Atlas carrying a presentation of the world on his shoulders, which faces visitors as they enter off Fifth Avenue. The reality and the myth of Rockefeller Center has had a powerful impact on my architectural sensibility. I identify it—architecture, not an architect, buildings and not a building—as my generative architectural influence.

My architectural milieu affords me a direct confrontation with the question: Does designing large-scale urban buildings, for those who use them as financial instruments of profit, diminish artistic resolve and promote inevitable compromise of ideas? This is a challenge that few of our master architects have risked taking. Rockefeller Center has proved itself a beacon, showing that there is a way, though tortured, out of this contemporary labyrinth. The status of Rockefeller Center as a masterpiece is undeniable; its architecture, evaluated solely through artistic merit, compelled me to study it more closely. Once within its embrace, one quickly understands that the process of design was as unusual and exceptional as the architecture it created. All those involved in this process were in pursuit of an ideal.

DENNIS GILBERT

ABOVE: **Pederson's DG Bank Headquarters, as seen from the Westend residential district.** OPPOSITE: **Nighttime view of the RCA Building (now GE Building) from the southeast.**

ADVANCE MEDIA DESIGN

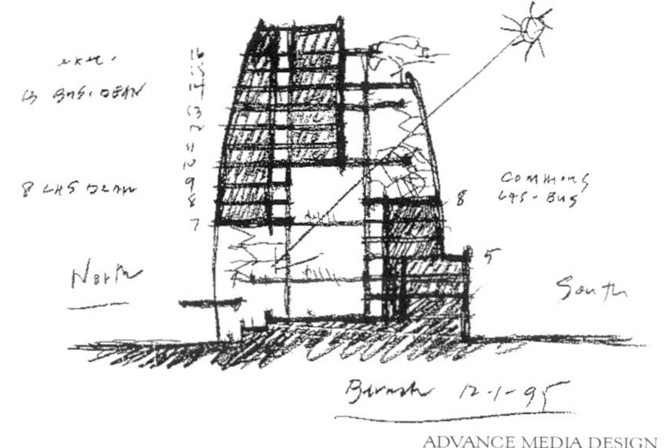

ADVANCE MEDIA DESIGN

Three views of Pederson's academic complex, Baruch College/City University of New York, 2001. ABOVE: Crosscut sketch. BELOW: Architect's model. LEFT: View of the interior.

ADVANCE MEDIA DESIGN

Each defined that ideal in somewhat different terms, each representing the other's definition. Above all, they realize the dynamic that sponsored their search was the juxtaposition of Rockefeller Center as a financial enterprise and Rockefeller Center as a work of art.

The architecture critic and historian Colin Rowe says that traditional architecture is largely focused upon the "internal angle" that creates form as embracing space. On the other hand, modern architecture, he says, is a product of the "external angle" that creates form as an isolated object. While outstanding examples can be stated to the contrary for both the traditional and the modern, one only has to look at the contemporary city to understand the condition Mr. Rowe is so neatly summarizing. Rockefeller Center, however, bonds the readings of buildings as figural objects and space as a figural void into a fluctuating state of coexistence, thereby resolving the conflict between the traditional and the modern condition. Most remarkably, the example set by Rockefeller Center was never followed. Soon after its construction, modern architecture took the stage, and its influence brought about the contemporary city. The city today is largely a collection of unrelated structures standing alone with littler regard for each other and with less regard for effectively shaping space into a larger public realm. The propensity in the modern city for isolated architectural events is further exacerbated by the fact that most urban structures are high-rise buildings. Once, during a more romantic period in our history, these buildings were called "skyscrapers," a term

BARBARA KARANT

Pederson's 333 Wacker Drive, Chicago, Illinois, 1983. View from across the Chicago River.

that engendered visions of the poetic possibilities inherent in their type. Now, a few take claim to such ambitions. At best, we can only refer to them as tall buildings. What is our modern city, if not predominantly an assemblage of large-scale structures of commercial sponsorship?

PERIOD
YALE VISITOR

Cesar Pelli

on

Eero Saarinen

I KNEW EERO SAARINEN WELL. I went to work for him in August 1954, just after I graduated from the University of Illinois when his office was quite new, and I worked closely with him in the design of several of his projects until he died in September 1961. I remained in the firm after his death and saw completed two colleges for Yale University, the project I had been working on when he died.

Most buildings designed by Eero Saarinen are very well known, but his contributions and intentions are usually ill-understood. No book was written on his work after his major buildings were built. One reason for this apparent lack of interest may be because Eero Saarinen did not pursue the consistent personal style that would have allowed his work to

SUSAN GRAY/OVOWORKS

SUSAN GRAY/OVOWORKS

be instantly recognized and to serve as a useful reference defining a particular way of giving form to buildings. We regularly use well-known images as mental illustrations in our conversations and writings, or to categorize architectural forms for ourselves or for others. In this respect, Eero Saarinen failed us. His search for appropriate forms was too ample to fit in any one formal category. But clearly, the purpose of architecture is not to provide us with tools of discussion or thought. This is just a convenient by-product. The value of an architecture resides at other levels: for example, in how well the individual building responds to its site and to the needs of its users, how much pleasure it gives us, and how its design contributes to the discipline of architecture.

To analyze and understand the contributions of an architect like Saarinen requires considerable work and thought. He had what was probably the most advanced design office at the time. Many of his processes have been seeping slowly into general practice. His office also provided an unusually successful learning environment. The record of its "graduates" attests to this success. I was deeply influenced by his example. In his office, I did not acquire a set of forms, but I learned to love the whole process of creating good architecture. His buildings followed a consistency of thoughts and not of forms. Consistency of thought is more impor-

PREVIOUS SPREAD: **Saarinen's interior of the Ingalls Hockey Rink, Yale University, New Haven, Connecticut, 1958.**

ABOVE AND LEFT: **Two views of Pelli's Canary Wharf Tower, England, 1991.**

tant, but also much more difficult to analyze. Architecture is a public art, and its practice presupposes responsibilities to the place and purpose of buildings, to users, clients and society, and to ourselves and our ideals. The hardest and most necessary thoughts in architecture address the difficult interaction between our responsibilities and our artistic goals. I do not remember Eero Saarinen ever discussing his general theoretical concerns, but I saw in his design process a consistent preoccupation with answering the demands of both his responsibilities and his art. Today, I have come to see that responsibilities are not hurdles, but essential parts of the unique art of architecture.

Saarinen did not help us understand him because he wrote little about his work. He was not inclined to verbalize his theoretical concerns, although he was very clear when giving design directions. He was a superb draftsman and he usually preferred to sketch his ideas rather than explain them. He has left us almost no guides to his sprawling body of work. To understand him well, we need to analyze each one of his buildings separately and to search for what was consistent in his motivations and guiding thoughts. To write well about him is, therefore, difficult, much more difficult than it is to write about his contemporaries with well-defined esthetic approaches, such as Louis Kahn, Paul Rudolph, or I. M. Pei. It is a pity that no serious scholar has attempted a good analysis of his work, because he has contributed much to our profession and in manners quite different from those of other well-known architects of his time.

To understand him, one should probably start by noting that Eero Saarinen was a committed modernist. He believed, like almost all architects of his generation, that modernism was the answer to a necessary new architecture. Everyone then understood by modernism, the architecture that grew from Le Corbusier's writings, the Bauhaus teachings, and the examples of a small core of architects. The forms of this modernism were codified as the International Style in the 1932 exhibition at the Museum of Modern Art in New York. Saarinen fully accepted the goals and discipline

Pelli's sketch of the North Terminal at Washington National Airport, Washington, D. C., 1997.

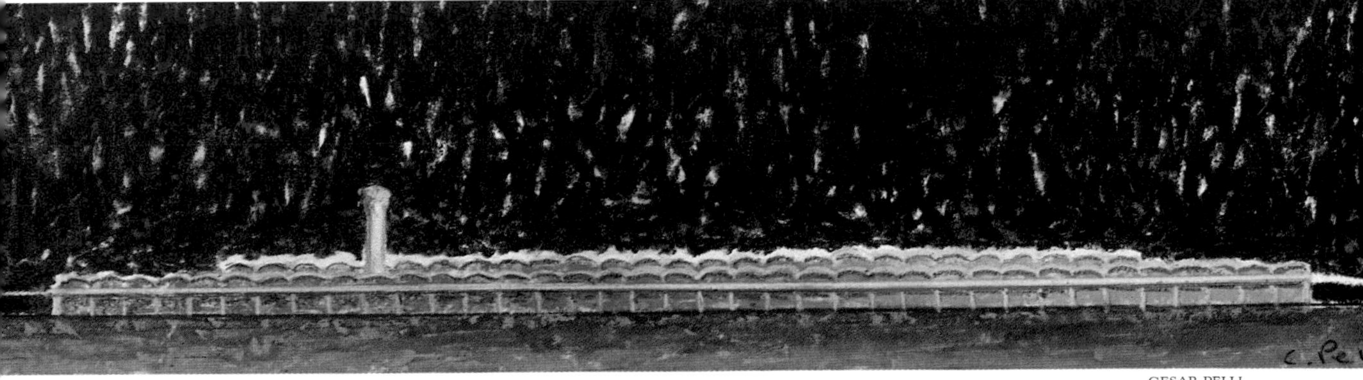

CESAR PELLI

of international modernism, but he also felt strongly that architecture needed to expand its formal limits in order to become truly universal and to be able to respond to all human needs and aspirations. His work can be seen as a form of exploration, probing multiple ways to resolve what he sensed were the shortcomings of modernism as practiced at that moment. I see my work also as explorations on the different issues each project presents me with.

He was one of the first modern architects to conclude that the "style" (his word)—the formal characteristics of a building—needs to adjust to fit appropriately in a given context. The particulars of the context include not only the well-accepted considerations of climate orientation, function, and scale, but also matters such as character, tradition and symbolism, which were normally ignored by modernist architects of his time.

Each building was for Saarinen an opportunity to experiment with new forms, ideas, and technology. He knew that his approach required taking risks, and in his work we find some aesthetically awkward buildings among many strong pieces of architecture. I worked closely with him as the project designer of the buildings for Ezra Stiles and Samuel F. B. Morse Colleges at Yale University, and they may provide us with a suitable example of his design process and architectural goals. These buildings are good but imperfect designs and, because of this, perhaps easier to learn from.

OPPOSITE: **Interior of Pelli's North Terminal at Washington National Airport, 1997.**

Saarinen's Samuel Morse and Ezra Stiles Colleges at Yale University, New Haven, Connecticut, 1962.

Saarinen was engaged in 1958 to design two new residential colleges for Yale University that were to be the eleventh and twelfth colleges of the University. The system of residential colleges was instituted at Yale in the early 1930s. They are typically two-to-four story structures, enclosing a courtyard, and housing 200 to 300 students in individual rooms or in small suites. Each college has its own dining room, library, lounge, a few rooms for games and hobbies, some classrooms, and two or three apartments for faculty members. Each college has a house for the master, who lives there with his or her family. The colleges are considered the center of social life of the students at Yale and have been purposely designed to encourage social interaction and exchange of ideas among students and between students and faculty. The college system is considered to be as important as the academic courses in the intellectual and social development of the Yale students

Saarinen had been an undergraduate at Yale and had great respect and love for the institution. He thought that the 1930s collegiate Gothic and Colonial buildings that housed the first ten colleges provided a very successful environment for undergraduate life. He particularly admired Branford College of 1932, designed by James Gamble Rogers, and this was the building he used to measure his work against. He had an estimator calculate how much it would cost to build Branford College in 1959 dollars. The answer was $100 per square foot—Saarinen's budget was $22 per square foot. He knew, therefore, that to compete in quality of materials and craftsmanship was impossible. The site that he was given was also less than ideal. It had the virtue of being across the street from the magnificent Payne Whitney Gymnasium of 1930 designed by John Russell Pope, but it was separated from the rest of the campus by a block of marginal shops. He was concerned that this location could isolate the new colleges and make them seem as less than fully Yale. The irregular shape of the site and its limited area were also obstacles, as they did not allow him to design the new colleges with simple plans around traditional rectangular courtyards.

Typically, we started the project by coming from Michigan to New Haven to visit the site and exist-

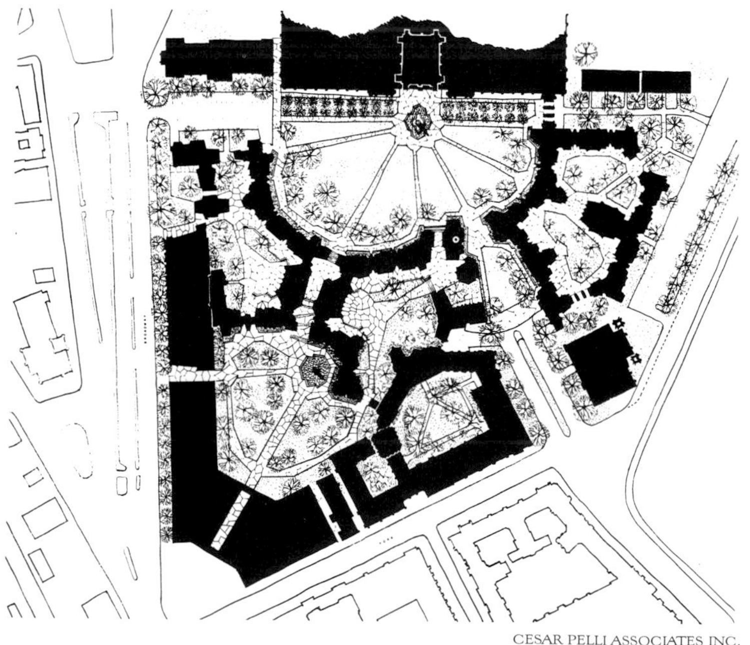

CESAR PELLI ASSOCIATES INC.

Site plan of Samuel Morse and Ezra Stiles Colleges at Yale University.

CESAR PELLI ASSOCIATES INC.

Scale model for Samuel Morse and Ezra Stiles Colleges at Yale University.

ing colleges, to talk with many students, some masters, and key administrators. We then analyzed dozens of possible schemes in plans and models, evaluating the pros and cons of each one. Saarinen rejected many schemes, such as high-rise slabs, for not being appropriately conducive to undergraduate life and not providing suitable places for casual encounters and exchange of ideas; others were too rigid or too expensive or did not respect the Gymnasium. At the same time, the office conducted several experiments on possible adaptations of contemporary technology to build an affordable wall with similar tectonic qualities as those of the old stone masonry colleges. A special large-stone, poured-in-place, pressure-grouted wall with the right look and feel was developed, tested, and selected. It was a very economical wall.

Saarinen believed that one of the responsibilities of this new project was to give the Payne Whitney Gymnasium an appropriate forecourt and a pedestrian, collegiate connection to the center of campus. He was also preoccupied with the issue of character. He wanted to design modern buildings and he knew that "character" was not a modernist concern, but he wanted his buildings to be able to give young undergraduates a suitable physical background for their dreams and hopes, buildings that would be as fully accepted and successful as those

PAUL HESTER

CESAR PELLI

ABOVE: West elevation of Pelli's Herring Hall at Rice University, Houston, Texas. LEFT: Pelli's sketch of Herring Hall, 1984.

of the earlier colleges. He also felt that his buildings, although modern, needed to connect with the collegiate Gothic architecture that gives Yale University its physical identity, so that the students living there could feel fully part of the University. He tried to develop abstracted forms sympathetic to the existing Gothic structures. He also believed that sculptures had contributed much to the richness of forms of the collegiate Gothic colleges. With a similar intention, he engaged Constantino Nivola to sculpt some thirty carved-in-place concrete pieces for the walls and courtyards of Stiles and Morse, and Oliver Andrews to forge sculptural light fixtures for the dining halls and for each stair entry.

Saarinen had designed earlier the Ingalls Hockey Rink of 1958. He had not felt then that the location or function of the hockey rink required that its architecture be tied to the Yale tradition. A hockey rink building on a busy street could be an exception or an exclamation point. But residential colleges presented him with a different responsibility. The forms that finally developed are not quite like those of any historical collegiate tradition nor are they part of any formal discourse of the time. Saarinen invented his own personal model. The forms of Stiles and Morse Colleges are an artistic synthesis of an amalgam of memories of Saarinen's years at Yale, medieval villages in Italy and France, collegiate buildings in England, and country buildings in his native Finland combined with his sense of appropriateness and modernity. He was searching for the right character. He knew that by fulfilling what he saw as his responsibility, he was courting severe criticism from the architectural press and, indeed after his death, when the buildings were finished, many writers reacted to his design with undisguised anger. In the 1960s, international modernism was still asserting itself, and many architects and critics considered that deviations from the canon by a well-known architect were unforgivable. Others understood his intention and considered this project an important model, opening doors to a richer and more expressive modernism. For a few years several buildings were built around the country imitating the forms and technology of Morse and Stiles Colleges.

The buildings for Stiles and Morse Colleges were built in time and within their budgets. They were finished in 1962 and have long ago become normal parts of the Yale fabric of buildings. The Payne Whitney Gymnasium now has a magnificent exedral forecourt that gives it a presence it never had before. The pedestrian walkway that connects the gym to the center campus runs between the two colleges and over the common kitchen. It is a very much used path and is one of the most often photographed picturesque views of Yale. The popularity of Stiles and Morse among their sister colleges has waxed and waned with the times, but they have always been seen as equal to the more traditional colleges in the center of campus, and the students of Morse and Stiles Colleges have always felt themselves as fully part of Yale. What Saarinen saw as his main goals and responsibilities were fully achieved. These buildings are early and important examples of a serious effort to adapt the principles of modern architecture to respond to the specific circumstances of a place with a strong architectural tradition.

James Stewart Polshek

on

Louis I. Kahn

GEORGE HOWE, WHO WAS Dean of the Yale Graduate School of Architecture during my first year as a student (1951–52), had brought two maverick teacher/architects to the University. One of them, Eugene Nalle, had an immense impact on my education. The other, Louis I. Kahn, influenced me only minimally during my school years, but his influence became increasingly significant in the ten years after my graduation. I first set eyes on Kahn in my second year at Yale. I noted, as did my fellow classmates, this shy, scarred, rather small man always wearing a bow tie. Next to my drafting desk under the dormers of the red sandstone faux Gothic Weir Hall, a young woman named Anne Tyng was building a strange rhomboid structure. Tyng, who I soon realized was Kahn's protégé and collaborator,

JULIUS SHULMAN, HON. AIA

kept to herself, focused intensely on the task of building a model of Kahn's theoretical structure (City Tower, 1952–57, unbuilt). Kahn would wander into our studio to chat with Tyng from time to time, but was quite reserved and not at all given to small talk with students.

Howe, a patrician Philadelphia architect, who self-mockingly referred to his Main Line stone residences as "Wall Street Pastorale," had broken with tradition with the design of the Philadelphia Savings Fund Society (with William Lescaze). His architectural modernism found a parallel in his progressive mentoring. He had allowed Eugene Nalle to create a radically experimental curriculum modeled on the Bauhaus, ITT and Taliesin—seemingly inconsistent pedagogies. This curriculum drew from the Bauhaus its interdisciplinary and collaborative traditions; from Mies van der Rohe at ITT the Jesuitical rigor of Cartesian grids and the strict vocabulary of materials and details; and from Taliesin both an attraction to the occult and a deep respect for the art of representational drawing. The program was an eclectic mix, sometimes confusing but always stimulating and so radically different from the enervating Beaux Arts orders I had studied in my first year at Western Reserve University in Cleveland before I transferred to Yale.

Nalle dominated my first two years in the program. Kahn became my critic in the first term of my fourth and final year. They were not "easy" teachers. Their pronouncements were often arcane and esoteric. And neither had built much so there were few available precedents. Nalle introduced us to architecture in a systematic way; Kahn did not. He was an inscrutable critic. No small talk, no long parables—only succinct aphorisms. I remember clearly his coming by my desk, looking down at a site plan on which I was working, and saying "Trees don't grow in rows." I retorted immediately, "They do if you plant the seeds in a row." He "harrumphed" and stalked off. Apparently, my Ohio pragmatism did not mesh well with Kahn's cryptic pronouncements; I didn't receive another crit for weeks.

I had completed two years under Nalle and his disciplined team, who were literally "hands-on"—often modifying our drawings in the wee hours of the night when we students were asleep. We worked in nearly windowless studios, buoyed by the cultural camaraderie that accompanies the nervous enthusiasm and close quarters of the early studio years. It was a shock, therefore, to move into Kahn's first major building, the Yale University Art Gallery (1951–53), with its fixed glass walls and its exposed tetrahedron structure. That my studio master had designed the building was itself intimidating; in addition, Kahn himself was unapproachable, absorbed with his late-blooming professional career, and distracted by splitting his time—geographically and personally. Despite his unorthodox appearance, his foreignness, and his radical background, he had been discovered by Yale's art historians, and his lionization had begun. In particular, Vincent Scully, who had been influential in Kahn's having been awarded the Yale University Art

PREVIOUS SPREAD: **Kahn's Salk Institute of Biological Research, La Jolla, California, 1965.**

Exterior view of Kahn's Yale University Art Gallery, New Haven, Connecticut, 1953.

MANUSCRIPT & ARCHIVES, YALE UNIVERSITY LIBRARY

Gallery commission, proceeded to create a "cottage industry" of the man.

In reflecting on those early years, I have realized how close to the mark writer Barbara Flanagan's 1991 impressions of Kahn's academic manner came to my experiences:

> The promise of a method—defined by Kahn's maxim if not by a handbook—reassured students that they, too, could make transcendent spaces and meet Kahn's challenge. Whether cruel or innocent, Kahn's promise was duplicitous. He intimidated students with the religiosity of his artistic process, but worse than that, he probably inhibited as much work as he inspired. (*Metropolis*, December 1991)

I never believed that Kahn intended to be cruel. Given the forces at work on this virtually unrecognized fifty-three-year-old, it is not surprising that his teaching would be affected. That he was not terribly attuned to students' insecurities in no way diminishes his enormous stature as an architect. And the reverse is true of Eugene Nalle—that he was not a great builder did not diminish his brilliance as a teacher of architecture.

In 1973, a year after becoming dean of Columbia University's School of Architecture, Planning and Preservation, I received a call from Marshall Meyers, an architect in Kahn's office, informing me that Kahn had died unexpectedly and alone in New York City and had not been identified for three days. Marshall asked if I could be of assistance to Kahn's wife, Esther, who was on her way to New York. I picked up Mrs. Kahn upon her arrival and escorted her to the city morgue, where she identified her husband. A few weeks later we held a memorial service at Columbia at which a number of Kahn's former colleagues, students, and, of course, Vincent Scully spoke. Kahn's having been propelled back into my life so dramatically was emotionally affecting.

JULIUS SHULMAN, HON. AIA

ABOVE: **Exterior view of Kahn's Yale University Art Gallery.** BELOW: **Kahn's Yale University Art Gallery (Sculpture Garden).**

MANUSCRIPT & ARCHIVES, YALE UNIVERSITY LIBRARY

It caused me to reflect on the extent to which I had indeed been influenced by his beliefs and his work. It also caused me to question whether the "classical" mantle that some art historians had posthumously conferred on him was legitimate.

In the nineteen years between my graduation from Yale and his death, Kahn and I had a friendly if intermittent relationship. During this time, I had apprenticed in three different offices, had established a practice, developed an academic career, and raised a family. My practice really began in 1963 in Japan with the commissioning of a basic research laboratory near Tokyo for a large Japanese corporation. This building was completed in 1965, and before its construction documents were complete, I was asked to begin designing a second one—an applied research laboratory between Kyoto and Osaka. At this time, I was not aware of Kahn's Salk Institute (La Jolla, California, 1959–65), but uncannily—either through coincidence, synchronicity, or unconscious influence—the formal, organizational, spatial, and systemic principles of Salk Institute and my Japanese projects were remarkably similar. There must have been something about Kahn's ethos and his work that I had consciously or unconsciously absorbed and re-expressed in these two early buildings. This affinity has, over the years, led me to try to find out how aspects of his life, his values, and his architecture might have influenced me.

Until Kahn died, I had not known much about his background. When I read that he was an Estonian immigrant whose father was a noncommissioned paymaster in the Army, I wondered what I, an American son of a middle-class businessman from Ohio, could possibly have in common with him. For one, I discovered that we were both Jews brought up in nonobservant families. (Mine, in fact, was almost assimilationist; my father, who was born in Hungary, was a politically progressive anti-Zionist.) For another, both of our mothers had been amateur musicians as young women (and in my mother's case an early feminist as well). Perhaps this is why we both were questioners of authority, progressive in our politics, and suspicious of theory. Louis Kahn's secular "Jewishness" has always interested me because I see in it the roots of his political and architectural radicalism as well as the basis for his interest in numerology and topology. And while I am personally far more sympathetic to his radical (i.e., rational) instincts than to his mystical (i.e., intuitive) ones, they are, in both of us, two sides of the same coin. I believe it was the tension between these two forces that gave him the strength to create an architecture that was more about "asking questions" than "giving answers," as Kahn in Talmudic spirit would phrase it, and that imbued his professional life with a powerful moral imperative. Like me, he executed few private houses, and his other work was almost exclusively for cultural, educational, scientific, or governmental entities. And although a full generation apart, we were both educated in the Beaux Arts tradition, deeply influenced by Cistercian architecture—Thoronet in particular. It would take a separate essay to speculate in detail about how Kahn's Jewishness affected his architecture. One does not have to look far to discover, in his form-making, the importance

RICHARD BARNES

POLSHEK PARTNERSHIP

TOP: **Polshek's Center for the Arts Theater at Yerba Buena Gardens, San Francisco, California, 1993.** ABOVE: **Rendering of the Center for the Arts Theater at Yerba Buena Gardens.**

Polshek's Rose Center for Earth and Space, American Museum of Natural History, New York City, 2000.

RICHARD BARNES

of cabalistic numerology (Tyng); the absence of "graven images" and consequent celebration of abstraction; the expression of monotheism in the circle in the square; and the Torah-like forms of Sher-e-Bangla Nagar, Dhaka, Bangladesh (1962–83), The Salk Institute, and the Performing Arts Theater in Fort Wayne, Indiana (1959–73).

The Kahn building I know best is the Yale University Art Gallery. This was Kahn's first major work of architecture and my last educational habitat. The simplicity of the building's central formal idea belies the complexity of its successful fusion with the adjacent Gothic revival building by Edgarton Swartwout. Not only does it respectfully complete the public face of the Chapel Street block front between York and High, but the new building also engages the site behind, responding sensitively to the changes of level. I watched the load testing of a single structural bay of concrete tetrahedrons, which occurred prior to actual construction, and realized then that Kahn's interest was principally in the geometry of construction rather than the affect of the completed work. Next to structure, Kahn was passionate about light. This is evidenced in the Yale University Art Gallery by the way in which Kahn fragmented the building envelope—completely glazing the west wall and cladding the windowless south wall in brick. We students experienced blinding sunsets through these fixed floor-to-ceiling windows, and in a move predictive of the aluminum foil on the windows of the towers at Richards Medical Research Building at the University of Pennsylvania (1957–65), we often covered them with tracing paper to filter the heat and light. But, of course, in this urban addition whose principal façade faced south, the architect was left with the Hobson's choice of reversing the opaque and transparent façades in the interest of environmental correctness or respecting the historic street front.

The resolution of these kinds of conflicts has become the leitmotif of many of our firm's buildings as well. Seamen's Church Institute (New York, 1991), the addition to Columbia University Law School (New York, 1996), Center for the Arts Theater, Yerba Buena Gardens (San Francisco, 1993), Queens Borough Public Library (New York, 1998), Rose Center for Earth and Space at the American Museum of Natural History (2000), and Scandinavia House, New York, New York (2000) are exemplary with respect to the resolution of rational orientation and contextual imperatives. I suppose the ultimate influence that Kahn's work and life had and continues to have on mine is the recognition that classicism and modernism need not be in conflict. Similarly, social and environmental responsibility and highly refined form-making can coexist. The resolution of these and other contradictory conditions has and will continue to define and energize the work of our firm.

BRUCE FLEMING

Model of COPIA: The American Center for Wine, Food and the Arts, Napa, California, 2001.

Antoine Predock

on the

Alhambra

IT WAS WHEN I WAS a student traveling in Spain on a motorbike in the 1960s that I first encountered the Alhambra. I had a limited understanding of Moorish architecture, since at that time architectural history courses to which I had been exposed barely touched on non-Western models. This moving, unforgettable encounter revealed a spatial realm that inalterably affected my path in architecture.

In Granada, there is a particularly heightened sense of the deep cultural strata of Andalusia, focused for me in the haunting presence of the gypsies. I had read the gypsy ballads (*Romanceros Gitanos*) of Federico García Lorca and felt a content and spirit in his work that both transcended and informed his powerful imagery. This intangible content was

ANTOINE PREDOCK

PREVIOUS SPREAD: **Court of the Lions, the Alhambra, Granada, Spain, 1338–90.**
ABOVE: **Court of the Myrtles.**

something that I also have sensed in examples of the architecture of Louis Kahn. In Lorca's Havana Lectures, he exposes the notion of "*duende*"—a charged state that one associates with the highest, almost mystical, levels of flamenco performance that I sensed had become an aspiration in his poetry. At face value, the Alhambra, born in the atmosphere of Granada, is a charming organization of gardens; but I would suggest that its riveting presence, so compelling to a casual tourist or aficionado, can be characterized as an expression of *duende*, as articulated by García Lorca and omnipresent in the flamenco "*Cante Jondo*" of Andalusia.

For me, the essence of any great building of any time—from Chartres to Ryoan-ji to Salk—is that ineffable power, that *duende*, that haunts whatever programmatic, cultural, or theoretical premises underpin its conception. In my work, although I aspire to these levels of spirit in architecture, I have found that *duende* is not a readily deployable "ingredient" that can be conjured up at will. It just shows up if I am lucky (or blessed) and of course, is in the (inner) eye of the beholder.

I will recount my journey of memory through this great masterpiece and perhaps make relationships to works of mine executed in the more than three decades since my first visit to the Alhambra.

Begun in the middle of the thirteenth century by the great Muhammad ibn al-Ahamar and finished 100 years later by Yusef Abdul Hagig, the Alhambra is a composite of sequential spatial perfection and layers of detail, formidably executed by Moorish master artisans. The Alhambra doesn't have an obvious "front door" (as has amply been pointed out about my Nelson Fine Arts Center in Tempe, Arizona). Rather, there is an immediate sense of the prioritization of nonhierarchically linked spatial sequences with the linkages *cum* chambers, for me, as charged as the "star" spaces they serve. These shadowy transitions to open courts never suggest an overly de-

Interior of the Alhambra.

ANTOINE PREDOCK

TIMOTHY HURSLEY

termined intention about entry, rather a quietly "morphing" condition in total contrast to the Platonic sequencing of the renaissance palace of Carlos V, which is intrusively embedded in one flank of the Alhambra. In an intention similar to the Alhambra, my Nelson Center eschews an emphasis on a linear procession, but rather is a multidirectional urban "filter." As the pageant of the progression of the courtyards of the Alhambra unfolds, each one has diverse perimeter definition: axially positioned chambers focusing views to distant landscape and multistory elements with interspersed towers. Many of the transitional spaces are relentlessly lined with calligraphic script carved in plaster, azulejo tiles or wood alfarge ceilings. All follow the repetitive principle of "zelige," so that they *become* surface and are not merely a decorative admixture. Verdant and arid courts thermally induce air movement from one to the next, and water in many guises seductively guides the procession. The "*Sol y*

Predock's interior of the Nelson Fine Arts Center.

TIMOTHY HURSLEY

ABOVE: Panoramic view of the exterior of the Nelson Fine Arts Center, Arizona State University, Tempe, Arizona, 1989. BELOW: Sketch of the same.

ANTOINE PREDOCK

ANTOINE PREDOCK

ABOVE: **Predock's Spencer Theater for the Performing Arts, Alto, New Mexico, 1997.**

OPPOSITE: **Predock's model of the Agadir Palm Bay Resort, Agadir, Morocco, competition, 1990.**

Sombra" of Andulusia in general and of García Lorca's bullfight in particular permeate the phenomenological matrix. This duality of sun and shadow has long since become a part of my work as it has evolved in the high desert of New Mexico. The journey through the Alhambra incorporates both subtle and complex level changes. Towers connect panoramically to sky and horizon while introverted subterranean realms like the baths are laced with rays of light. The choreographic imperative in examples of my work, like the Turtle Creek House, Dallas, Texas, unconsciously parallels the sectional elaboration and displacements of the Alhambra. Also, the sense of the palace/fortresses' roughly articulated outer shell contrasting with its delicate inner lining is present in my Danish National Archive scheme.

It is an interesting closure for me to realize that two of the most powerful and personally influential epochs of architecture, the French High Gothic and the Anasazi works of the American Southwest, are roughly contemporary with the Alhambra. All share that baffling quality, that *duende*, that charges great architecture over time. One of its notable residents, Washington Irving, characterized the Alhambra as "one of the most remarkable, romantic and delicious spots in the world."[1] To that I would add that the Alhambra, residing in that realm of myth and spirit so powerfully articulated by García Lorca, extends the experience of architecture far beyond the merely picturesque.

And they're entering a labyrinth.
Love, crystal and stone.[2]

1 Washington Irving. *Tales of the Alhambra.*

2 Federico García Lorca. *Poema del Cante Jondo.*

ROBERT RECK

Raj Rewal

on the Unknown Architect of

Fatehpur Sikri

I HAD GONE TO FATEHPUR SIKRI for the first time at the age of eighteen as a young student of architecture. There were thirty of us, and we had stayed for three days on the out houses of the complex. At that time I was intrigued by two aspects of Fatehpur Sikri. One was the different manners of supporting sun shades, "*Chajjas*," by stone brackets. I had sketched on the site more than ten different ways, each one of them elegant construction details carried out with meticulous craftsmanship. Why such a lot of different ways for doing the same thing in one building complex? If God is in detail, as Mies had said, I presumed that constructors of Sikri believed that there were many ways to reach the God, and they were not stuck on one minimalist detail or dogma. The other thing that seemed to intrigue me was the often-repeated fact that emperor Akbar, the builder-owner of Sikri, could not read or write and that the name of the architect of Fatehpur Sikri was not mentioned in the records of the period.

Twelve years later I went back to Fatehpur Sikri as a young professor with my wife and friends. We had taken several trips, staying in the Dak Bungalow on the ridge. At this period I was fascinated by the different manner of constructing the roof over different chambers in Fatehpur Sikri. How the square rooms were converted to octagonal or sixteen-sided base before the construction of domes was initiated remained a perpetual source of pleasure. I was able to explain easily my enthusiasm for the construction techniques and principles of squinch arches or corbelled stone spanning the corners to my nonarchitect wife, as the building methodology is clearly visible and expressed with honesty in sandstone. Five-storied Panch Mahel's construction in Fatehpur Sikri with point leads of stone columns, beams, and slabs is at least three hundred years ahead of its time and anticipates present-day prefab techniques.

This was also a period when I had just started my architectural practice and was building my first houses. The clients were a mixed lot—a well-known politician, editor, and painter, et al. In each case, the final decision about the placement of rooms and func-

HELENE AND RAJ REWAL

PREVIOUS SPREAD: **Fatehpur Sikri's sun shades in stone.** ABOVE: **Five-storied Panch Mahal construction in sandstone overlooking Pachisi court, Uttar Predesh state, N. India.**

HELENE AND RAJ REWAL

Fatephur Sikri: "at least three hundred years ahead of its time."

tional requirements was taken by their wives. The editor was not even informed that his library would be hidden away in the basement! The painter, who happened to be deaf, was the most articulate, but even his wife had the final say. It began to dawn on me that perhaps Fatehpur Sikri's planning owed more to Akbar's wife, Jodhabai, than to the illiterate Akbar. She was a princess of the Jaipur state and a learned woman. One of the components of Fatehpur Sikri is still named after her as "Jodhabai Palace," and its planning owes more to earlier buildings in Rajasthan than anything I had seen in Afghanistan or Uzbekistan, from where the Akbar's mogul predecessors had come.

Fatehpur Sikri is built on the indigenous principles of living with the climate according to the seasons. The resultant forms are based on courtyards, roof terraces, and deep verandas. The roof terraces with "Chatris" umbrellas are utilized for outdoor sleeping in summer nights or for winter afternoons when the inner rooms are cold.

The tradition of building in sandstone is specific to the region of Rajasthan and Gujrat, and the mogul methodologies of building domes in brick were experimented with original fervor in sandstone with great elegance and originality. Surely Princess Jodhabai may have influenced some aspects of planning, but the constructivist principles of Fatehpur Sikri can only be attributed to the architects and craftsmen.

MADAN MAHATTA

MADAN MAHATTA

Truth to the materials and structural clarity are important features of Sikri long before modernists claimed it as their credo. My own work was influenced by the underlying principles of honestly expressing structure and materials but built in concrete and brick. The staff quarters for the peons of the French Embassy built in 1969 were successful enough to land me larger housing projects. Based on a competition, I was awarded the Permanent Exhibition Complex of Delhi. This was a space frame in concrete, and its inspiration was as much the works of Nervi as the su screens of Fatehpur Sikri.

Within the next decade I was dealing with larger commissions where external spaces in the form of courtyards became a major element of design in my works. I felt I had imbibed these values consciously or unconsciously from Fatehpur Sikri. I was always

HELENE AND RAJ REWAL

TOP: **Rewal's Permanent Exhibition Complex, New Delhi, India, 1974.**
ABOVE: **View across the courtyard of Fatehpur Sikri.**
OPPOSITE: **French Embassy, staff quarters, New Delhi, India.**

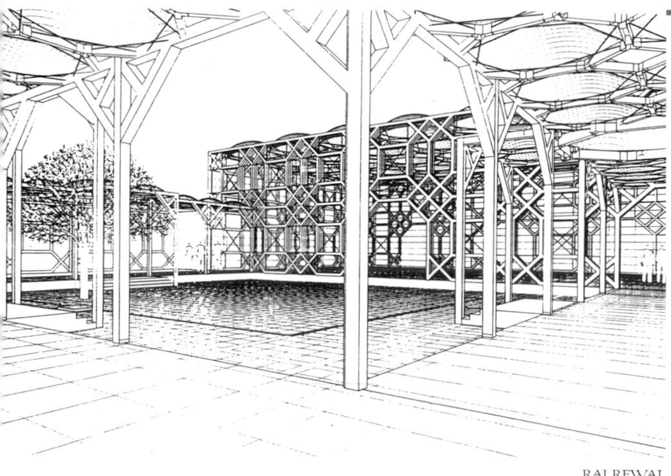

RAJ REWAL

View of Jamatkhana through the Cloisters, Lisbon Ismaili Centre, Lisbon, Portugal, 1999.

deeply touched by the sequence of spaces within Pachisi Court at Fatehpur Sikri. They provide a changing panorama to the visitor. The paved court allows orientation in different directions, creating different perceptions of the reality of space and form. It was also a period when my clients tended to be "building committees" often dominated by finance members. If driven to the wall, I could always appeal to the poetic sensibilities of one or two members to achieve desired architectural results. But the final decisions were generally taken by the finance member or the invisible force.

The idea that a vast organization had to have a

committee prompted me to think that Akbar must have delegated the responsibility of overseeing the design of Fatehpur Sikri to his council of "nine jewels" (that's what his Council of Ministers were called). Perhaps an illiterate monarch is not different from an anonymous organization that works through committees.

Historically it is well established that Akbar was open-minded, tolerant, and adventurous. He was shrewd and encouraged discussion amongst his courtiers, and by listening to debate between persons of diverse opinion he acquired knowledge and wisdom. He had a creative interpretation of Islamic, Hindu, and Christian religious views and founded a new creed called "*Din-E.Ellahi.*" It can be safely assumed that such a person would encourage new methods of building from diverse sources.

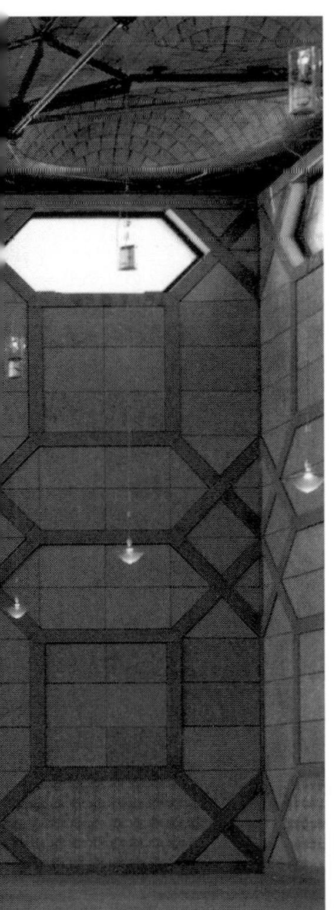

HELENE REWAL

Interior view of the Ismaili Centre.

Fatehpur Sikri has the most liberating sense of space and displays an amazing intermingling of internal and external enclosures. There are no fixed routes in Fatehpur Sikri, and modulation of spaces is carried out in a subtle manner. I was deeply intrigued and influenced by this aspect of Fatehpur Sikri in my middle years. It seems to me important that liberty of movement is granted to the visitor and perception of space realized by each individual in his own manner. These are the qualities I associate with modernity, each one finding his path in his own way.

While grappling with the design of Lisbon Ismaili Cultural Centre four years ago, I began to view Fatehpur Sikri in a new light. My major problem was to discover symbolic values that would have common connections between Portuguese traditions and the Aga Khan's progressive Ismaili community living in Lisbon. I wanted to express in a state-of-the-art structural system the inherent Portuguese and Ismaili heritage. In this respect I was inspired by Fatehpur Sikri, where purity of structural principles is maintained, materiality of stone is valued, and the structural systems have a dual role of pointing towards deeper symbolic connotations. Akbar's Fatehpur Sikri points the way towards synthesis of architectural concerns, which we value today. Its modernity is informed by timeless liberal ideals of tolerance and freedom of architectural expression. Akbar, being illiterate, had a fresh approach and was

HELENE REWAL

OPPOSITE: **Assimilation of Iberian architectural heritage in the ceiling of the Ismaili Centre's Jamatkhana; utilization of local stone.** ABOVE: **Photo of the completed roof.**

probably more open to bold ideas than ambiguous Hamlet—"To be or not to be"—and this certainly helped to formulate the design of Fatehpur Sikri.

The structural systems in stone in Fatehpur Sikri are lighter than masonry construction elsewhere and can be compared to contemporary reinforced concrete buildings, where the walls are redundant and the loads are carried only on columns. In comparison to Sikri, Lutyen's New Delhi Imperial Complex or Corbusier's Chandigarh Capital Complex appear rigid. Only a warrior king may have demanded a light building in stone comparable to the tents he used as camps in warfare. Fatehpur Sikri is a unique combination of building in stone fused with a mind-set used to living in tents.

The name of the architect for Fatehpur Sikri may remain a mystery, but one can safely assume that the tradition of building in a hot climate was adopted through Princess Jodhabai, the program of building enclosures with diverse functions through the Committee of Nine Jewels, and the adventure of building in stone from the unknown architect and craftsmen who gave the form. Perhaps the synthesis of all these values may well be attributed to the high spirited, illiterate, wise monarch who took risks and encouraged creativity.

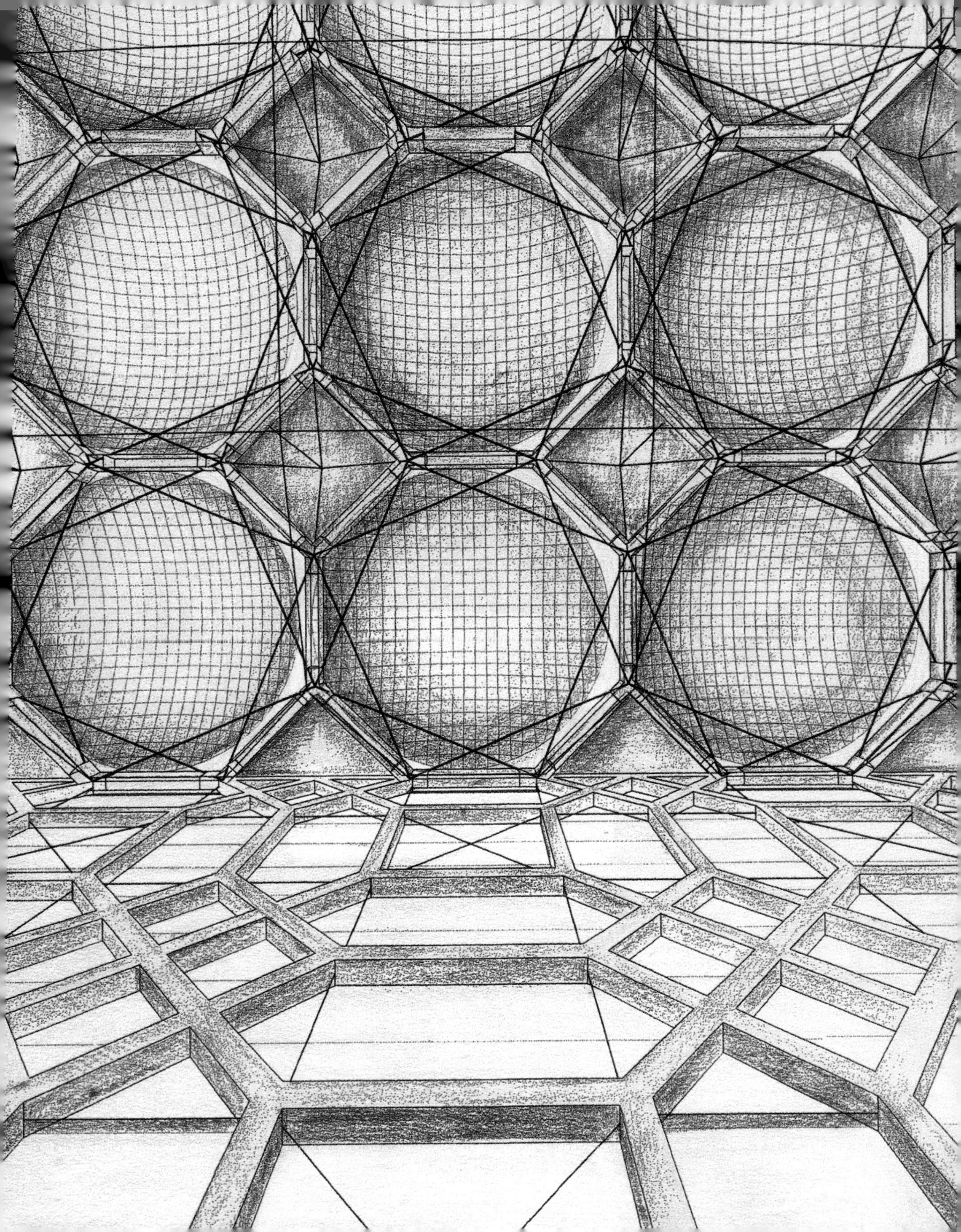

Richard Rogers

on the

Maison de Verre

"Flowing to the sea, the river remains faithful to its source."
—AN OLD FRENCH SAYING

IT WAS IN 1955, when I was a student at the Architectural Association, that I was first introduced to the Maison de Verre. It was to become one of the most influential buildings that I had visited in Europe, for the architect, Pierre Chareau, had expressed a wholly new and original vision of the modern house and had managed to perfect its execution.

At the time, the British architectural scene was utterly dominated by the tradition of Le Corbusier, Mies van der Rohe, Gropius, and Alvar Aalto. I myself had strayed

JORDI SARRE

somewhat from the norm and added the genius of Frank Lloyd Wright to my list of architectural demigods. Isolated as we were during the war years, by the early 1950s only a handful of people in Britain knew about the Maison.

My recollection is a little hazy, but it was either James Stirling or Peter Smithson, both my tutors, who had told me about the Maison. It was, however, my friend the architect/sculptor, Tim Scott, who got me in to see the house and meet the original clients—the Dalsaces—who had commissioned their close friend, the architect and designer, Pierre Chareau to design the house together with Bijvoet and Fers Doubert.

I ended up writing my thesis on this marvelous project, which had totally captivated my imagination. I consequently returned to the house, took poor photographs, drew poor drawings, prepared poor texts, and eventually to my great surprise saw them published in *Domus*, in what was conceivably the first postwar article on the Maison de Verre.

Since then I have become friends with their grandson, Marc Vellay; quite fortuitously, the son-in-law of Vellay was my wife, Ruthie's, obstetrician. When we were building Beaubourg, we regularly visited their house, and he delivered my son, Roo, in 1975.

In 1931, the Bernheims had bought their daughter, Anne Dalsace, an eighteenth-century *hotel particulier* (a residential building that wraps around a courtyard) and hired Pierre Chareau to redesign the building. At first Chareau intended to tear the building down, but the upstairs tenant would not move, so he inserted the house under the tenant's apartment. Since Chareau was primarily a furniture builder, the house became a kind of built-in cabinet. Hence his constraints became his creative fuel.

Since the courtyard did not get much light, Chareau had enclosed the house within two walls of opaque brick glass—a sandwich of a sort—with glass on the front and glass on the back. At that time, the technology for the glass brick that Chareau had used was only six months old; it was a huge risk to use it as a building material because the manufacturers were not guaranteeing its reliability.

The façade of the house is rather deceptive. From the outside, it looks as if it would be a large house, but it is actually rather small. Everything in the Maison de Verre has its place and function. Nothing is hidden—what you see is what you get.

The front door of the Maison de Verre is not in the front at all, but rather to the side, so one has to abruptly turn to enter the house. The placement of the doorbell also has a radical orientation, as it is on a separate post a few feet away from the entrance. The route from the front door to the first-floor, double-height living room is one of the great wonders of modern architecture. You enter to be faced by a transparent, lightweight steel staircase—one of the most beautiful staircases of the twentieth century. To reach it, you move though a series of

PREVIOUS SPREAD: **Interior of the Maison Verre, Paris, France, filled with daylight.**

JORDI SARRE

Night view of the exterior of the Maison de Verre—the house is again filled with light.

light-diffusing metal gauze doors. The breathtaking, double-height living room filled with diffused light is the heart/culmination of the building.

We have preconceived ideas through our past recollections and associations of what we expect a building or a room to look like. The Maison de Verre challenges all of them.

My fascination with the Maison de Verre was on many levels—the magnificent space, the way you move through the space, the innovative use of new materials, and, above all, that amazing soft light which infuses space. It was the light that was the most amazing thing—a magical mixture of direct and diffused light, something that I have never seen before.

At night, huge external spotlights theatrically light the outside glass walls of the Maison de Verre. The glowing light magically leads one towards an open stairway and then on and up to the salon. The house feels very much alive with its neverending spirals and labyrinths of perforated metal screens, steel, and glass. It glows with human-ness.

The Maison de Verre was completely modern, yet it was not part of any accepted tradition of modernism. It seemed to echo oriental elements similar to the sixteenth-century Japanese imperial palaces: fixed and mobile screens, sliding doors, minimalist and fixed furniture, opaque brick glass walls (rather than paper) that filtered the light.

The Centre Pompidou, built with my former partner, Renzo Piano, borrowed ideas from the Maison de Verre—the use of transparency and industrial components, enclosed escalators where the light filters through and leads one up towards an open sky, and the sliding doors that allow the exhibition space to be flexible and mobile.

Like the Maison de Verre, the Centre Pompidou has many familiar elements: bridges, ships, air-conditioning apparatus, mast, wires, and escalators that are both functional and symbolic.

ROBERT POLIDORI

Exterior view of the Centre Pompidou.

Both the Pompidou and the Maison de Verre have been compared to a yacht, a Japanese temple, and furniture cabinets. The Maison de Verre has also been compared to Marcel Duchamp's *Large Glass*—with the bride residing in the upper level or private living quarters and the bachelor residing in the lower level or the ground floor. The lower level was where Dr. Jean Dalsace had his clinic, which may have been the first unofficial family-planning center in France—a very radical idea at the time, for birth control was still forbidden.

When the Centre Pompidou was built in the 1970s, the architecture was thought to be radical. But to us, it represented a symbol for openness and change. The Centre Pompidou was built first as a people's museum.

Architecture can re-energize a space—act as a catalyst, so to speak. For example, my Millennium Dome in London is a very old and primitive form, but it was built with new technology and therefore it is not an example of mass and volume (i.e. the Pantheon) but a lightweight structure whose superimposed transparent layers create its form—a flexible nonbuilding. The Millennium Dome is not a self-supporting structure, as with some of Buckminister Fuller's domes, but a suspended structure like the beautiful Brooklyn Bridge in New York. The masts of the Millennium Dome are also similar to the supporting girders of a bridge.

ROBERT POLIDORI

ROBERT POLIDORI

Two views of the exterior of Rogers's Centre Pompidou, a "people's museum," Paris, France, 1977.

A dome is a very efficient structure. In other words, the forces are all balanced—everything is in harmony. "Harmony," by the way, was a favorite word of Chareau. The sphere has the least amount of the external area in relation to the amount of space inside; in other words, very economical. Like the Maison de Verre or Duchamp's *Large Glass*, a double theme can exist—the sky above, covering the earth; the upper and the lower spheres; the head on top of the body; the masculine and feminine spaces. There is spiritual meaning, as there are many different religious beliefs associated with the domical shape.

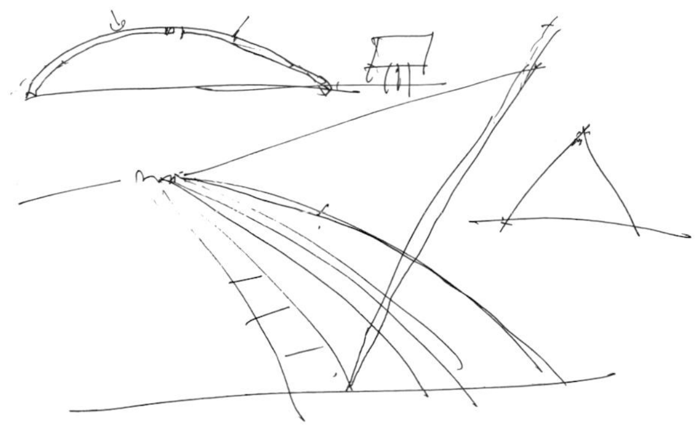

RICHARD ROGERS

SUSAN GRAY/OVOWORKS

The translucence that had been provided by the glass in the Maison de Verre was the type of translucence that I sought for the Dome. However, the material I used is completely different and extremely technologically advanced—a rolled version of Teflon and fibre stitched together with steel. I've used two skins: an external weather shield, which is stretched tautly to the steel mesh of the suspended castle system, and an internal layer—gently, undulating, and softening the underside of the Dome.

The Maison de Verre is more than a house—it is an idea about living and about how things are made. Chareau had the chance to carry out his idea through to the minutest detail. If you look at the details of the girders, you realize they're as important to him as the layout of the living space itself. Everything has an important role to play, and all the parts come together to strengthen an idea. Nothing is hidden, everything is exposed—the electrical wiring and plumbing hardware. The industrial ventilation system with its wheels and cranks and pulleys are proudly displayed as if they were a piece of art.

Chareau was immensely innovative. His work depended on an entirely *artisanal* approach, in a time where the machine, mass-production, and materialism

ABOVE: **Sketch of Rogers's New Millennium Dome, Greenwich, England.** LEFT: **View of the structure from across the water.**

ruled. I am sure that the chemistry between architect, designer, his team, and clients was critical—in fact, Chareau never produced such great art again. Inscribed on the outside wall of the house are the words: "Pierre Chareau 1931; COLL-Bijvoet; fers-Dalbert, rue Saint-Guillaume"—signed as if the house were a piece of art, which of course it is. The Maison de Verre, with its handcrafted industrial simplicity, became a very complex idea and like a piece of art, holds different meanings for different people.

The glass house has affected everything I've done. Even in my own house in London, I have borrowed and reworked Chareau's ideas: translucent screens that divide the living room, the eating area, and the bedroom; steel girders that stand upright in the middle of the room, an obvious homage. All I need are bookshelves and a piano, and I guess I have it. Of course, you never copy, but if you saw the staircase in my house you would see how important the Maison de Verre is to my whole approach.

My fascination with the Maison de Verre at another level was that there was a sort of handcrafted technology—the way it was made to look as if it had been factory produced—when actually everything, from the doorknobs to the lamps, to the bath and shower doors, to the large structural elements, was handcrafted and custom wrought. Each and every object had its own individual and idiosyncratic details conceived from first principles; nothing was left to whim and everything was executed to reflect Chareau's overall vision. Chareau had clear input to each and every object in the Maison de Verre. Although the house looked as if it were machine assembled, each element was hand produced. All were connected, overlapping to create a harmonious whole.

Chareau was unrecognized by the mainstream, but he was watched carefully by the leading architects of the time. There is a story that while Le Corbusier was building the Maison Savoie, he used to stop and examine the progression of the Maison de Verre while it was in the process of being built. The Maison de Verre is engineered, a "Rolls Royce," if you like, whereas Corbusier's Villa Savoie is very much one piece of concrete sculpture.

It is not a question that one is more beautiful than the other—they are both beautiful. It is fascinating that, in a way, they are both completely modern but they are very different from one another.

I suppose I take chances up to a point, but I try to minimize risk. You have to take risks or you do nothing—you would never get out of bed if you were safe all the time. Like Chareau, my aim is not so much to be an innovator but to achieve a certain perfection—to perfect my idea, my statements of beliefs, principles, and opinions. Like Chareau, I believe that the social aspect of things is of prime importance. Chareau built the Maison de Verre when the prevailing ethic was a production ethic—a time to buy, to consume without worrying about future consequences. His handcrafted technology was an idea, a statement that architecture should enlarge life, not reduce it.

Chareau's philosophy enriched my vision of what and how architecture could be. Ideas should be radical in the sense that you push yourself to find

Rogers's Lloyd's of London building, London, England, 1986.

new things, to explore, to discover—not just for the sake of discovery itself but for helping mankind to live a more fulfilling life.

Architecture, like life, is a learning process. And here the word "process" is important, as it implies movement and change. Often the idea one starts with is not what one ends with. The important issue is to use the constraints set by regulations, etc., to strengthen, not weaken, the idea. In order to do that you have to have fluidity. You have to be able to move with it. You can't be rigid about your approach—you have to understand what the constraints are and then solve the problem afresh. And, if you're lucky, if you're clever, you might actually improve the design because of those constraints. I always say to students, take from it strength—turn the problem on its head and make an advantage of it.

My K-1 Ikura building in Tokyo was the first building in Japan to have intumescent-paint fire protection. The external steel structures allowed

SCOTT GILCHRIST/ARCHIVISION

the use of small-diameter columns as opposed to the traditional steel-reinforced concrete frame. This enhanced the transparency of the building. Nippon Steel used the Ikura building to promote their fire-rated steelwork. With the courage of my client, I was able to use technology to improve and liberate lives.

There's no one way of doing something, but we must work together with nature. We now understand much more about the damage that we have done. We tend to do things for today and fail to see the damage that we are creating for tomorrow. But we have to live tomorrow and our children have to live tomorrow, so sustainable development implies taking into account the future in whatever decision you make today.

I've had the Maison de Verre in my mind for a long time, but I don't refer to it all the time—perhaps only occasionally. As you get older, you refer less directly. You absorb more. I have to absorb things. That's how I work.

But above all, the Maison de Verre is a supreme demonstration of innovation and open-mindedness. Chareau reviewed every element down to the minutest detail and reinvested it in the light of the possibilities presented by the new materials and new manufacturing techniques. Nothing was taken for granted; everything was up for grabs. The brilliance of the result is a testament to his supreme virtuosity, his collaboration with artisans, and the incredible support of a committed client.

In many ways, Chareau's achievement at the Maison de Verre symbolizes for me the power of innovation itself. In today's world, a world where we are beginning to recognize the damage we are inflicting on our environment and our children's futures, the Maison de Verre stands as a challenge to our complacency and moral apathy—a shining demonstration of the power of the human imagination and its ability to create positive change.

Richard Rogers's essay was based on an interview with the editor, Susan Gray, in the House of Lords, London, England.

Rudolph's Sarasota High School, entry steps, Sarasota, Florida, 1957–59.

DER SCUTT

Der Scutt *on* Paul Rudolph

WE WOULD ALWAYS KNOW when Rudolph was coming up the stairs to the office at Thirty Five High Street. He had this rapid pitter-patter of a step. Of course, one had to ascend quickly and in a straight manner, as there were no hand rails, which would have cluttered the appearance of the narrow entrance stair.

Rudolph's physical appearance didn't

change much in the forty years I knew him. His carrier-top flat crew cut never seemed to grow. His thin, black, knit tie with Ivy League knot was either worn every day, or else he owned more than one black tie. The tie could never show the black ink stains that must have come in proximity to the millions of lines laid down by him.

Rudolph was never into fancy clothes. He frequently wore a gray tweed jacket with white shirt and never an undershirt, and always seemed to have a hole in his left rear trouser pocket, worn through by his little wallet. He frequently had bigger holes in his shoe soles. He never wore a hat, or a scarf, or boots, or rubbers in snow or rain.

It was my privilege to work for Paul Rudolph during my student days at Yale, followed by four years of full-time employment. I was one of the few whom he trusted to make the ink-line perspectives.

Rudolph worked on the same type of sloping board as everyone else. The Rudolph-designed drawing board, loose on custom legs, was not always prone to remain in position. His favorite position was to sit on his stool with his right leg crossed over his left leg at a rigid right angle.

There were ten drafting positions and one secretarial table in the office on two sides of a thirty-five-square-foot plan, with a sunken pit in the center. A large wall served as a pin-up surface to review drawings. Project design crits took place in the pit, as did all meetings with clients. The favored few got to sit on well-worn puffy brown leather cushions. Others sat on the pit's edges on the lambskin rug, parts of which would usually cling to one's trousers, especially if they were flannel.

No one had privacy in telephone calls, including Rudolph. We all could hear every conversation he had with anyone and everyone. He was always serious and businesslike. Occasionally he would joke about someone's lack of drawing ability or miscomprehension of a detail. Those who could faithfully follow his design intentions lasted the longest. He was impatient with incompetence and generally held engineering consultants in high disdain. He would point the finger at them with utter mistrust and foredoom their inability to think three-dimensionally; he called them mundane pipe-and-duct people. He thought city planners did more to destroy cities than any other force.

He never paid a Christmas bonus, and his annual Christmas message was to stomp out, usually around three o'clock in the afternoon on December 23, without a word to anyone. He would go directly to his apartment to play the piano shortly thereafter. Other times, usually on weekends, he would fill his grand living area with sounds of lyrical pleasure, but almost never in front of friends or anyone. He was quite musical and accomplished at the piano. I could frequently hear the music as I walked past his apartment to the rear parking lot.

The greatest opportunity one could have with this mannered genius was to witness the evolution of a design. His yellow paper sketches, large or small, were electrifying with ideas, images, and interior wonder. His ability to draw and express his visions on paper was fast and furious. Discarded ideas would fly into the wastebasket occasionally, and even those sketches were rich in architectural excellence. As those infrequent discards weren't meeting his exact vision, he would

OPPOSITE: **Rudolph's Boston Government Service Center, 1962–71.**

HELMUT JACOBY

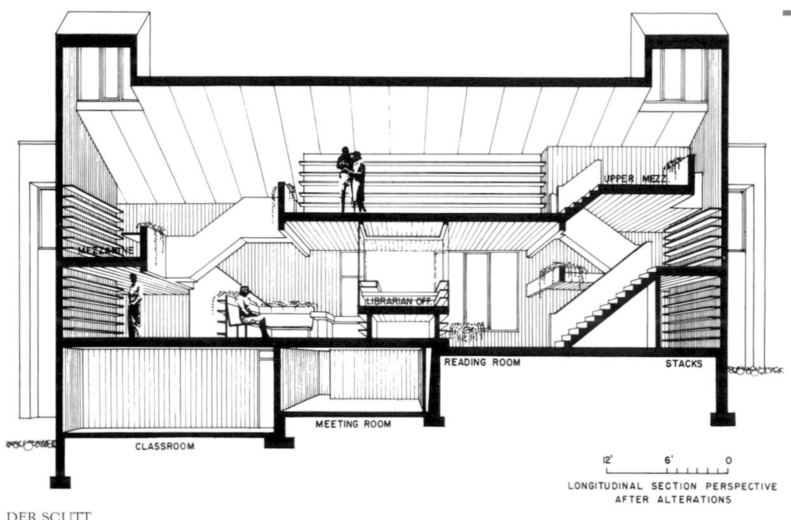

DER SCUTT

ABOVE: Rendering of Scutt's Barlow School Library, Amenia, New York, 1964.

BELOW: Scutt's International Flavors & Fragrances headquarters, Hazlet, New Jersey, 1989.

ROY WRIGHT

continue to explore. Like Wright, he thought a lot about his next building before he drew it. His drawings feel and express three-dimensional space, always with a spontaneous stamp of artistic sensation.

Mies would make a purist box without event; what saved the Miesian interior or exterior mass was his faithful and precise conclusion of proportions. Rudolph, on the other hand, was dedicated to making spaces with all sorts of appendaged events. Interlocking and overlapping forms both vertically and horizontally provide visual interest and spatial variation. His understanding of space and procession is unparalleled by most architects.

Aalto, who learned from Le Corbusier, and Kahn, who learned from the Greeks, are two of the twentieth-century heroes who understood light. Rudolph's Corbusian influence of light in architecture is obvious. Rudolph's acute awareness of shade and shadow, of light on the exterior fragmentation of form, was remarkable. Wright understood it, but I absolutely feel Rudolph took it further. Kahn was the only other contemporary of Rudolph to also create unique architectural statements involving play of light.

Mies never solved turning the corner, and Rudolph joked privately, "Only Wright knew how to turn the corner." And Rudolph was always quick to praise Wright for knowing where the front door is.

Rudolph was famous for his tiradical crits to Yale students. "I can't find the front door—and you don't understand scale!" he would lament. Many students were totally intimidated and destroyed by Rudolph's crits. He was intensely direct and quickly cut to the issue. Rudolph's pedagogy, unlike that of many other teachers, indelibly marked his students. He never tried to influence the Yale students with his style and unique approach. He taught space, invention, and principles.

When Rudolph designed a stair, it always had flair. It would rarely be straight. It would have curves and lacy endings, beginnings, and wraparounds. Almost inevitably, the riser-to-tread relationships were in conflict with building code mandates. The processional ascent or descent was not without a glorious ambience and impact!

His architecture was clearly inventive and unique. He despised two-dimensional banality. He never bisected an architectonic element; he always put the focus at the third point of the composition from which architectural energy sprang. The nips and tucks, the cantilevers, the slants, were always synergizing into a harmonious whole of explosive delight. Flat surfaces could never exist without a restless spirit.

He loved making original shapes that sparked a kind of musical syncopation. His love of bright colors clashed with rough beton, but at the same time made the raw concrete quietly become soft and subservient. He understood plan and mass composition in a way that was impossible to duplicate. One can copy Mies, emulate some Le Corbusier, and replicate some Wright ideas, but no one can copy pure Rudolph!

Rudolph replaced Mies's sterility with convincing elation. He will always be remembered for his ink drawings. Watching him start and work on these incredibly tantalizing images was seeing audacious creativity at its best. Every line described the evolution of space and the carefully considered control of light. The areas of ink line intensity and thick-

972-9400

ness varied to expose rusticated textures in concert with reflections and pools of dramatic accent. It was like cooking Piranesi into a voracious, lyrical ecstasy. The drawings resembled Piranesi with bells and whistles. His plants hung straight down as if weighted. His shimmering water looked and felt wet. His cape men, as we called them, looked like figures from outer space, and only he could draw them; I was severely scolded once when I tried to copy these scale figures.

He was very shy, and just when you thought he had stage fright, he would emerge as a brilliant orator with an abundance of clear, intelligent observations. He was continually thinking and questioning. Rudolph's manipulation of spatial variation influenced my modest Barlow School Library renovation of 1964. Juxtaposing seven-foot-high spaces with the thirty-four-foot-high central reading area dramatized majesty with low-scale intimacy. My introduction of light in unexpected places created a vibrant interior ambience.

The large circular garden walls of my International Flavors & Fragrances household products headquarters in Hazlet, New Jersey, create a strong image for a building sited in a large grass field. The exterior shapes gave signal that a structure with special purpose is poised for corporate promise. These giant wing walls contain required structural seismic bracing, and shelter and frame flowering gardens for enjoyment by the building's occupants. Rudolph frequently employed geometry and bold massing to exert visual interest and contradictions. Sometimes his forms perched with delicate balance, and other times they met their foundations with passion and force.

My Corinthian condominium structure in Manhattan is a building Rudolph thought was my most exciting project. He wrote to the AIA College of Fellows Committee in 1987, "Der Scutt's condominium on 38th Street is undoubtedly one of the most distinguished buildings in New York City."

The Corinthian's semicircular vertical column forms evolved from wanting to give every occupant a dramatic vista of Manhattan from each living room. The dramatic column forms act like pistons at the tower's top.

Rudolph would always meet the skyline with a sculptural crenellation of some kind. His restless massing was always moving with a rhythmic energy full of visual purpose. The shade and deep shadows of the Corinthian's massing contributes to making a huge fifty-six-story box become a structure that is pleasing to look at and live in. How many boring and banal, boxy residential buildings can we sustain until our urban fabric becomes senseless?

Rudolph most definitely ranks equally with Le Corbusier, Wright, and Kahn, four of the greatest innovative architectural geniuses of the twentieth century.

OPPOSITE: **Scutt's Corinthian, a fifty-six-story condominium, New York City, 1988.**

Robert A. M. Stern

on

Paul Rudolph

I FIRST GOT TO KNOW Paul Rudolph in the early 1960s at Yale when he was the chairman of the University's Department of Architecture and I was a student there.[1] Rudolph propelled Yale into a position of prominence in architectural education—and Rudolph's association with Yale, which led to three building commissions from the University, including the incomparable Art and Architecture Building, propelled him onto center stage in the evolving drama of postwar international architecture. Rudolph was very different from a typical Yale department chairman. He was brash, brusque in a way many found refreshing and many did not. Though genuinely shy, Rudolph was not inherently modest. He worked very hard at his architecture and at his teaching and he expected everyone else around him to do the same.

He was not scholarly in any way; in fact, it can be said that he lacked cultivation. The son of a Methodist minister, he was raised in a variety of southern towns before training at Alabama Polytechnical Institute (now Auburn University) and going on to Harvard's Graduate School of Design for two years in its master's class. At the time of his appointment to Yale, Rudolph had behind him a brilliant series of small houses, the majority built in Sarasota, Florida, and a succession of posts as visiting critic at a dozen or more mostly provincial universities. But Rudolph's career was blossoming: the Jewett Arts Center at Wellesley College, his first major work, was also arguably the first serious challenge to the uniformity and placelessness of the American version of the International Style that Walter Gropius and Marcel Breuer had advocated at Harvard in the 1940s.

Rudolph was an American pragmatist of the highest order. He did not have a theory of education, nor did he seem interested in developing one. Until Rudolph brought Serge Chermayeff to the school as a permanent faculty member in 1962, he seemed anxious to avoid theory of any kind. But Rudolph was intensely interested in the "learning process." Despite his lack of an interest in pure theory, he sensed that the art of architecture could not evolve without a higher sense of purpose—higher, that is, than the utilitarian functionalism and structural determinism (he labeled it "structural exhibitionism") of the day. In 1961 he wrote that "action has indeed outstripped theory and...it is the unique task and responsibility of great universities such as Yale to study, not only that which is known, but far more important to pierce the unknown. My passion is to participate in this unending search." While what Rudolph meant by "theory" was not clear from what he wrote or what he said in the design studio, it certainly didn't mean some critique of architecture's validity such as we seem to have today. I think he meant that architecture was not just problem-solving but an overarching act of will. His was an heroic view. Rudolph saw architecture as a supervening force: "We must understand that after all the building committees, the conflicting interests, the budget considerations and the limitations of his fellow man have been taken into consideration, that his responsibility has just begun. He must understand that in the exhilarating, awesome moment when he takes pencil in hand, and holds it poised above a white sheet of paper, that he has suspended there all that will ever be. The creative act is all that matters."[2]

Though Rudolph had no specific philosophy of education, he had a brilliant sense of architectural composition and a passion for formal invention that he was able to convey to students at their drawing tables and in the formal design juries on which he invited the most brilliant and successful architects of the day to serve, turning these events into major learning experiences and major milestones in the evolving architectural discourse. In

PREVIOUS SPREAD: **Rudolph's Yale Art and Architecture Building, Yale University, New Haven, Connecticut, 1963.**
OPPOSITE: **Rudolph's Jewett Arts Center, Wellesley College, Wellesley, Massachusetts, 1958.**

© PETER AARON/ESTO

Stern's Ohrstrom's Library, St. Paul's School, Concord, New Hampshire, 1991.

addition to his passion, Rudolph had a sense of urgency through which the education process became more stimulating, tense, and intense than it had probably ever been before.

The zenith of Rudolph's effectiveness as a teacher can be said to be the years 1960 through 1963, when his career as a practicing architect took off, when he worked intensely on the building that would become his masterwork, the new home of the Art and Architecture School, and when a brilliant group of students was attracted to the school where he taught in the advanced master's class for one semester each year and in the third-year studio in the other. Rudolph was a superb teacher; his analyses at reviews were trenchant, but his real forte was the one-to-one desk crit during which he could look at a primitive sketch and see things in it that its fledgling-architect author probably had not seen, or even could not see. He would talk to students as though they were colleagues. Nonetheless, he remained in charge; he could be very intimidating, especially at final reviews, when he would take no prisoners, particularly among those who substituted flashy presentations for serious thought. "Pretty drawings do not an architect make," he said more than once, leaving his fellow jurors and the student being reviewed equally speechless. But, if you had an idea, even though your drawings were bad and your model worse (and mine were), he would sway the jury with eloquent interpretations of what he felt was promised, what might develop.

The completion of the Art and Architecture Building in 1963 marked the watershed of Rudolph's career at Yale. The new building was a tour de force, a profound work of eclecticism within the modernist canon, bringing together the raw brutalist approach of Le Corbusier's late work with a sense of spatial intricacy that was a hallmark of Frank Lloyd Wright (whose Rosenbaum house had exercised a profound effect on Rudolph when he first saw it in his student days in Alabama). Despite its modernism, Rudolph's Art and Architecture Building was also remarkably sensitive to its context, playing beautifully to both Yale's many-towered Gothic townscape to which it formed a gateway, and to Louis Kahn's austere, somewhat inert Art Gallery across the street. But despite its sources and its contextuality, it was a building with a unique power all its own, inside and out. The Art and Architecture Building was dedicated on November 9, 1963. The "buzz" was very loud indeed, and hundreds of guests accepted the University's invitation to tour the building. President Griswold, who had done so much to make Yale a center of modern architecture, had recently died, and there was still a sense of loss despite the festivity of the occasion. But most shockingly, at the formal dedication ceremony, which was to be the highlight of the day, the keynote speaker, Sir Nikolaus

ROBERT A. M. STERN ARCHITECTS

Stern's Arts, Media & Communication Building, California State University, Northridge, California. Perspective rendering, 1999. To be completed 2001.

Pevsner, dean of British architectural historians, quite clearly made known his displeasure with the design. Pevsner was critical of its individualism, which he felt might thwart creativity, and he was clear-seeing in his concerns about the long-term effects of weather and intense use on the raw concrete that was virtually everywhere exposed, outside and in. In many ways Pevsner proved right, but those of us who were passionate about Rudolph and about the building couldn't (or wouldn't) see it.

Paul Rudolph left Yale in May 1965, moving to New York with high expectations for a brilliant career that did not quite work out as he hoped it might. His last jury was for the thesis class of which I was a member. So his departure from New Haven was mine as well (or so I thought) until I recently returned as the school's Dean, which has led me to think very often about Paul Rudolph as teacher and as architect. The lineup of panelists on that final jury was stellar, but not unusually so: as I recall it, Rudolph was joined by Serge Chermayeff, Robert Venturi, Vincent Scully, Philip Johnson, Ulrich Franzen, and Henry Cobb. I remember the clarity of thought, as well as the vitality and outspokenness of debate which went with that last day, a stark contrast to much of the self-congratulatory "feel good" discussion that so often passes for critical discussion inside architecture schools today. And most of all I remember my last teacher-student exchange with Paul, on the steps of the Art and Architecture Building, after the review was over, when he got yet one more well-intentioned jab in—complimenting me on my work, he faulted me on a less-than-forceful verbal presentation. Imagine that.

Paul Rudolph died in 1997, laid low by the hazardous effects of working with asbestos, a material he had discovered fresh architectural possibilities for while an officer in the Navy in World War II and had used extensively in his work beginning with the interiors of the Art and Architecture Building, where he sprayed the ceilings with it to provide an acoustically effective complement to the rough concrete walls. Until much later, in the 1970s, Rudolph, like most of us, was unaware of the lethal power of this "wonder" material.

Rudolph's career, so spectacular in its rapid rise, was sad in its steady decline in the 1970s and 1980s, accelerated by his sometimes cavalier attitude to sound building practice, but much more profoundly by the cultural shift that occurred in the aftermath of Kennedy's assassination and during the Vietnam War, when the heroic model gave way to one that valued the realism of the everyday. In this period, Rudolph, largely abandoned by American clients, was lucky enough to find opportunities abroad, mostly in Southeast Asia, where his work, though bold as ever, did not seem fresh in the way it once had. For ten years the media's darling, he was virtually ignored by writers after the publication of a monograph of his work in 1969. Now his Art and Architecture Building, once the symbol of an unbridled optimism, and later criticized for it, is being reappreciated. Its condition today is sad, having suffered a serious fire of suspicious origins during the strife-filled spring of 1969. After being reviled by Charles Moore, Rudolph's successor at Yale, it was so indifferently repaired that Rudolph refused to

© PETER AARON/ESTO

Stern's Smith Campus Center, Pomona College, Claremont, California, 1999.

visit it until 1988 when he returned for an exhibition of his drawings and to inaugurate a series of lectures endowed in his honor. Since that time the reputations of the Art and Architecture Building and its architect have grown and grown.

1 This essay was in part adapted from a talk, "Britons at Yale in the 1960s," delivered at the seminar *The Special Relationship: American and British Architecture Since 1945*, held at the Paul Mellon Centre for Studies in British Art, London, 29 October, 1998, which in turn was based on an earlier article, Robert A. M. Stern, "Yale 1950–1965," *Oppositions* 4 (October 1974): 35–62.

2 Paul Rudolph, "The Architectural Education in U.S.A.," *Zodiac* 8 (1961): 162–165, quoted in Stern, "Yale 1950–1965": 47.

Hans Busso von Busse

on

Paul Rudolph

IN 1954, IN THE new graduate class at the Massachusetts Institute of Technology (MIT), a motley group of budding architects had come together from all over the world—from the United States and Canada, from Britain, India, Italy, and Germany. One thing they all had in common was an obsession with architecture. Eighteen students, chosen on the strength of their success, wanted to study, together with their American friends, the building arts of that country, which at that time was regarded as the mecca of modern architecture. In the course of their studies, the young people also hoped to meet some of the leading architects of the day. Something occurred that would have been inconceivable in Europe: our esteemed and greatly revered teachers Dean Pietro Belluschi and Professor Lawrence B. Anderson engaged the elite of the architectural profession in America to conduct their own design seminars, which were each to last three weeks. The architects included Eero Saarinen, John M. Johansen, Minoru Yamasaki, Eduardo Catalano, Buckminster Fuller, and last but not least Paul Rudolph, who had just made a name for himself with a number of unusually fine houses in Florida.

One condition of this fantastic experiment

PREVIOUS SPREAD: **Cocoon House (Healy Guest House), Paul Rudolph with Ralph Twitchell, Siesta Key, Florida, 1951.** ABOVE: **Rudolph's Jewett Arts Center, Wellesley College, Massachusetts, 1958.**

was that the design projects of the architects invited to MIT had to be completed within three weeks. This meant working day and night for the whole semester. No one was allowed to abandon the task—but that was anyway a matter of honor for MIT students.

Paul Rudolph had announced his design seminar for February 1955, and the project was to be a beach house—good reason to study his houses in Florida in advance.

The Healy Guest House in Siesta Key, Florida was built in 1951. As in most of Rudolph's early works, the architectural form was determined by the structural elements. The distinguishing features of his architectural language are already evident in his early buildings. With the visible resolution of the load-bearing structure into its constituent parts, a powerful, initial articulation is achieved. This articulation creates a sense of scale. It also conveys an impression of the structural forces involved, the paths they follow, and the way they are resolved architecturally. This act of structural revelation is the first stage in a process of articulation in which the building acquires its sense of scale and proportion.

Paul Rudolph's buildings are structural depictions in which the aesthetic qualities of imaginative technology, balanced proportions, and an expression of playful lightness are brought out in masterly manner. In that respect, the design principles underlying the best Renaissance architecture are evident in his work—principles one may find in the Palazzo Rucellai by Alberti, for example, and in other Florentine palaces.

The compositional principles of Rudolph's design also reveal a second level of articulation that lends his buildings a sense of scale. This manifests itself in the remarkable complexity of the detailing, in the elements and jointing principles of the construction, and in the nature and surface quality of the various materials when seen in conjunction with each other. A typical example of this may be found in the Jewett Arts Center at Wellesley College. Pursuing a concept of "separation," Paul Rudolph resolves the rough, undifferentiated elements of the building into small-scale, complex systems: a thick column, for example, becomes an elegant cluster. In addition, he detaches the load-bearing columns from the non-load-bearing walls and, wherever structurally possible, separates the ceiling from the walls. The façade acquires an astonishing sense of scale through the layering it undergoes in response to the needs of constructional physics: a small-scale sunscreen system, for example, is followed by opaque and transparent façade elements set in a number of planes behind each other like a series of membranes. The underlying aim is to create a well-coordinated hierarchy of scales that defines the architectural image both internally and externally. This method enabled Paul Rudolph to organize a richly varied and complex sequence of spaces and to respond to different urban constraints and relationships in a most sensitive way.

The Jewett Art Center at Wellesley College, the Art and Architecture Building at Yale University in New Haven, the Married Student Housing project, and the Boston Government Service Center are all outstanding examples of his use of the principle of proportional hierarchies and articulation by means of separation.

HANS BUSSO VON BUSSE

Sketch of Charles Klauder and Frank Day's Greenhouse (1922) and Galen Stone Tower (1931), Wellesley College.

"Things are quite chaotic. We are faced with a vast change of scale, new building forms...."[1] With these words, Paul Rudolph laments the coarsening of architectural language and the loss of a sense of scale in modern architecture. There are many indications that his message and the example he set in his teaching have scarcely been understood by his contemporaries.

There is another aspect of his architecture that seems remarkable to me from a European point of view. The lack of expression of modern architecture and the sometimes arbitrary nature of its undifferentiated images, its ubiquitous stereotypes—the works of Helmut Jahn and many of his contemporaries spring to mind—are not attributable merely to a loss of scale. What is also missing is a readiness, an ability, a sensitivity on the part of many architects to come to terms with a specific "place" in their design work. No building stands in splendid isolation. All buildings form part of a complex urban or landscape fabric. Architecture cannot be reduced simply to the resolution of functional and economic problems if it is to contribute to the creation of a desirable environment. This aspect alone justifies its claim to be an art.

Special mention of yet another quality of Paul Rudolph's architecture should be made at this point. Where the architect Klauder used hand-worked stone to suggest traditional Gothic forms in the Wellesley Tower and the Green House, Paul Rudolph pursued a quite different path. He accepted the terms of the location and its neo-Gothic ambient as an expression of the tastes of former times. He was discriminating in his understanding of form, so that his design approach does not lie in a radical aesthetic opposition to the genius loci—something with which we are all too familiar from the ahistorical basic attitude of the Bauhaus. Paul Rudolph sought to establish associative formal links to the existing surroundings, using a modern, industrially inspired vocabulary of materials and forms. The aim is to combine new and old to create an effective new entity. In this respect, attention has to be paid to questions of scale, to compositional aspects such as series and order, to rhythm and proportion, to materials, surfaces and coloration, to the creation of urban spatial forms and the treatment of light, and to the silhouette of a building against the sky. In the new identity that the architect seeks to create for an urban situation, traditional-historical, psychological, and ultimately the unique mental and spiritual qualities of the discovered "place"—together with the modern forms he sensitively introduces—

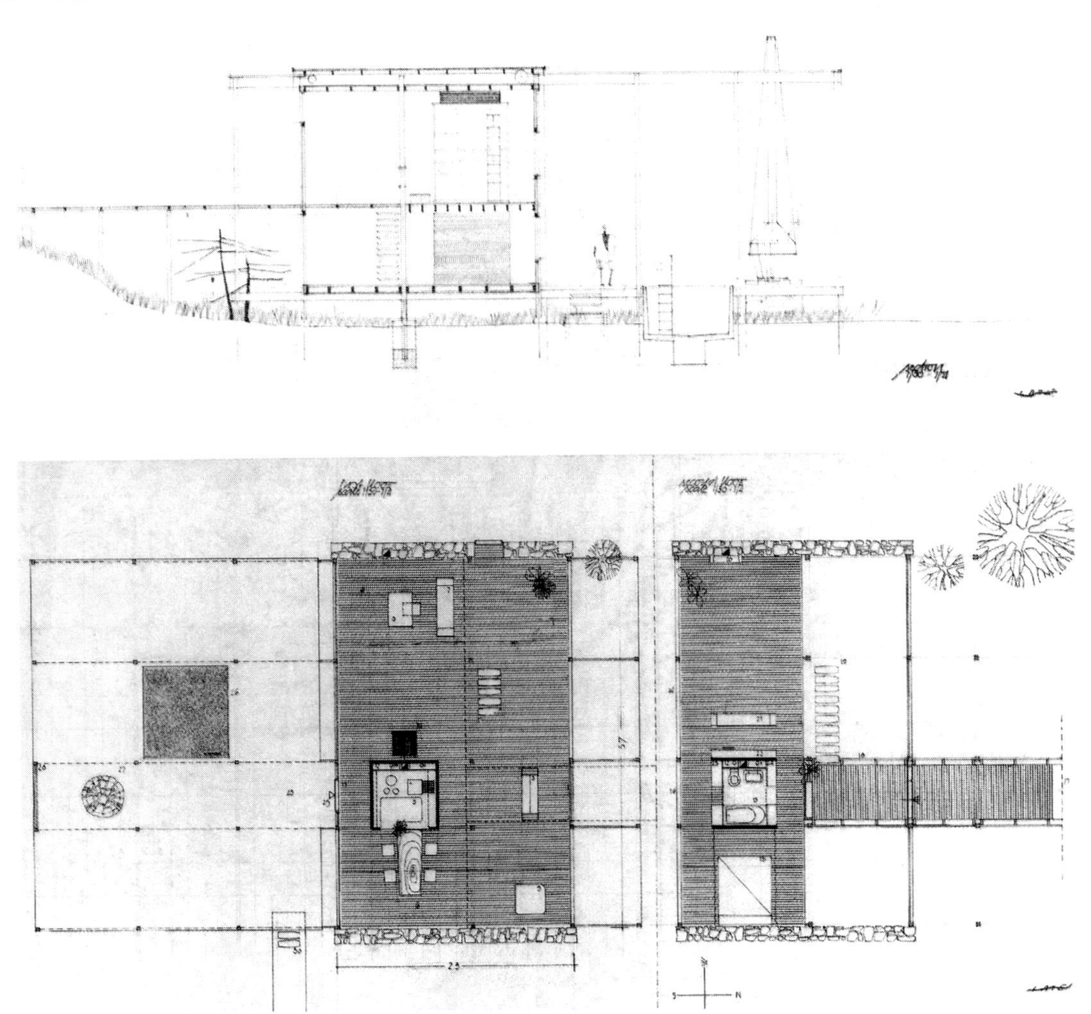

HANS BUSSO VON BUSSE

Rendering of the Beach House, Cape Cod, Massachusetts, 1954.

HANS BUSSO VON BUSSE

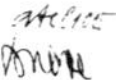

ABOVE: Rendering of the Beach House, Cape Cod, Massachusetts, 1954.

LEFT AND BELOW: Two views of House Tegernsee by Hans Busso von Busse and his son, Bernhard, at Lake Tegernsee, Bavaria, Germany, 1959.

© SIGRID NEUBERT

© SIGRID NEUBERT

will all find a mutual and genuine form of expression.

Good architecture, after all, always conveys a message. The architecture of Wellesley College, for example, allows us to experience the essential value of a recognizable link between tradition and history on the one hand and the present on the other. In this context, Paul Rudolph remarks:

> Making the entire environment of the city a more habitable, and indeed a more beautiful and significant place, is our real problem. . . . The role that a building plays in relationship to others, whether it is the focal point, turns the corner, or is a flanking building, must be clearly defined. This is always the point of departure, which any building must work from to give cohesion to an environment. . . . The architect has abdicated from his traditional role as civic designer, and tends to be concerned only with his individual building and site. Large-scale, three-dimensional design, as an integral part of what has gone before and what is likely to come, must be the province of somebody. I would call him an architect.[2]

Paul Rudolph's contribution to an extended, holistic understanding of the city and its historical substance cannot be rated highly enough. For far too long in this dynamic country, the traditional values of its architecture have been sacrificed to a concept of progress. The buildings of the first Chicago school that have been destroyed are a sad example of this. In contrast, I regard the revitalization of parts of the old harbor in the center of Boston, with its historical office and warehouse buildings, as a hopeful sign. It is no coincidence that the architect responsible for these measures, Frederick A. Stahl, was, like me, a student of Paul Rudolph. In a later generation, at least, there is a greater awareness of the public value of the architectural heritage.

Paul Rudolph was a person given to reflection. He sought the nub of every assignment, its specific, unmistakable character on which the architectural expression should be based. For him, architecture was the genuine, visual, and symbolic translation of the experiences and values of life into a form in which they could be communicated through no other comparable art medium. Architecture as language; architecture as sign and symbol, and as expression—Paul Rudolph, the teacher, convincingly communicates to us those aspects that were important to him:

> I have always been interested in the specific, and drawing from it whatever generalizations one might find. The universal space concept is a denial of the richness and complexity of life that architecture must celebrate. I want to accentuate the differences in our life, not nullify them. It is important, though, that universal spaces such as offices, manufacturing and commercial buildings read as such.[3]

In this representational aspect of architecture —in the message it conveys—beauty plays an indispensable role. Vitruvius describes the beauty that enables a work of architecture to move the mind and spirit of the observer, to delight and edify him; for the beauty of a space, of a building or an urban ensemble is capable of elevating our senses and emotions to a realm of perception and recognition. Of that, Paul Rudolph was also convinced.

© JENS WEBER

Exterior of passenger clearance area, Munich Airport (von Busse, Blees, Buech, Kampmann), 1992.

Through whatever form of art we encounter beauty of this kind—in poetry or music, in the visual arts or in architecture, and whether it elevates or illuminates us or makes its claim on us in some other way—beauty awakens insight in us, incites us to astonishment, and arouses deep emotions. It can afford us a perception of what is true, what is valid, and what is of enduring value in our existence. *Pulchritudo splendor veritas*—beauty is the splendor of truth.

Paul Rudolph was a great teaching personality. None of his students could resist his insistent train of thought, nor indeed did they want to. Discussions with him were always of the utmost intensity. Our fascination with him lay in the credibility and the captivating aura of his personality. Our days together at MIT began at eight o'clock in the morning. During the strenuous phase toward the end of the project when we worked day and night on our designs, it was not uncommon for him to take us away from our drawing boards, over which we had fallen asleep during the night, and we would end up in one of the pubs on Harvard Square. As far as our work was concerned, he was unrelenting; but he made up for this with his inimitable ability to motivate his students to outstanding achievements. In spite of all our cheerful toils, my memory of Paul Rudolph is of an inspired and gifted teacher.

My design for a beach house at Cape Cod gained

his approbation. He thought the questions of scale and the relationship of the house to the location had been properly resolved. He expressed his doubts about the use of stone rubble to the end walls. On the other hand, my drawings received his unreserved approval.

Two experiences I gained during that period of learning have had a lasting influence on my subsequent work: the concept of hierarchies of scale for building and space, and a concern for all aspects of "architectural place" relevant to a design.

If one takes a critical look at recent architectural developments in America, one sees that it would have been of great benefit to that country if the teachings of this great American architect and the examples he handed down had had a greater influence. I am all the more grateful for having had the privilege of making the acquaintance of this great teaching personality in my younger years. As a result, I was able to take back to Europe the best of the American architectural tradition as part of my equipment for practicing this fine profession.

—*Translation by Peter Green*

1 Paul Heyer, *Architects on Architecture* (New York: van Nostrand Reinhold, 1978) 295.

2 Ibid., 304.

3 Ibid., 303.

© JENS WEBER

Interior of passenger clearance area, Munich Airport (von Busse, Blees, Buech, Kampmann).

Selected Works and References

Diana Agrest

1945 Born in Buenos Aires, Argentina

1967 Diploma of Architecture, University of Buenos Aires

1967–69 Postgraduate studies at l'École Pratique des Hautes Études and the Centre de Recherche d'Urbanisme, Paris

1972–76 Taught at Princeton University, Princeton, New Jersey

1972–84 Fellow, Institute for Architecture and Urban Studies, New York

1980 Cofounded Agrest and Gandelsonas Architects, New York

1994 Founded Diana Agrest Architect, New York

SELECTED WORKS

1999 House in Madrid, Spain

1996 New Town, Shanghai, China

1995 Melrose Community Center, Bronx South, New York

1992 Hillside Residential Neighborhood, Des Moines, Iowa

Cranbrook Campus Gate, Cranbrook Academy, Bloomfield Hills, Michigan

Vision Plan, Des Moines, Iowa

1991 China Basin, San Francisco, California

1990 House on Sagpond, Sagaponack, New York

1988 Duplex on Central Park West, New York

1986 Deep Ellum Neighborhood, Dallas, Texas

1978 Park Square, Boston, Massachusetts

1977 Building I, Buenos Aires, Argentina

1976 Project for La Villette, Paris, France

1975 House for a Musician, Majorca, Spain

SELECTED PUBLICATIONS

1996 Coeditor, *The Sex of Architecture* (Henry N. Abrams)

1994 *Agrest and Gandelsonas Works* (Princeton Architectural Press)

1991 *Architecture from Without: Theoretical Framings for a Critical Practice* (MIT Press)

1983 *A Romance with the City* (Cooper Union)

PROFESSIONAL AFFILIATIONS

Professor, the Irwin S. Chanin School of Architecture, Cooper Union, New York

The Alhambra

ARCHITECTS
Unknown; built under Muhammed ibn al-Ahamar, founder of the Nasrid Dynasty, and his successors

BUILT 1338–90

LOCATION
Granada, Spain

TYPE Moorish palace/citadel

MATERIALS
Sun-dried brick (tapia)

Tadao Ando

1941 Born in Osaka, Japan

1962–69 Self-educated in architecture

1969 Established Tadao Ando Architect & Associates in Osaka

SELECTED WORKS

2000 Awaji-Yumebutai (Awaji Island Project), Tsuna-gun, Hyogo, Japan

Komyo-Ji Temple, Saijyo, Ehime, Japan

1997 TOTO Seminar House, Awaji Island, Hyogo, Japan

1995 Meditation Space, UNESCO, Paris

1994 Chikatsu-Asuka Historical Museum, Osaka, Japan

1993 Rokko Housing II, Kobe, Japan

1992 FABRICA (Benetton Research Center), Treviso, Italy

1992 JAPAN PAVILION EXPO '92 / SEVILLA, Seville, Spain

1991 Museum of Literature, Himeji, Hyogo, Japan

Water Temple, Awaji Island, Hyogo, Japan

1989 Church of the Light, Osaka, Japan

1984 Time's, Kyoto, Japan

1976 Row House, Sumiyoshi, Osaka, Japan

SELECTED AWARDS

1997 Royal Gold Medal, Royal Institute of British Architects

1996 Premium Imperiale

1995 The Pritzker Architecture Prize

1993 The Award of Prizes of the Japan Art Academy

1992 Carlsberg Architectural Prize, Denmark

1991 Arnold W. Brunner Memorial Prize, American Academy and Institute of Arts and Letters

1989 Gold Medal of Architecture, French Academy of Architects

1985 Alvar Aalto Medal, The Finnish Association of Architects

1979 Annual Prize, Architectural Institute of Japan

PROFESSIONAL AFFILIATIONS

Honorary Fellow, The American Institute of Architects

Honorary Fellow, The Royal Institute of Architects

Luis Barragan

1902 Born in Guadalajara, Jalisco, Mexico

1924 Graduated from the Escuela Libre de Ingenieros, Guadalajara; self-taught as an architect

1925–26 European tour

1932, 1936 Attended Le Corbusier's lectures in Paris, France

1976 Established a private practice in Mexico City, Mexico

Exhibition, Museum of Modern Art, New York

1988 Died in Mexico City

SELECTED WORKS

1976 Monumental Fountain for Lomas Verdes, Mexico City (with Ricardo Legorreta)

1972 Francisco Gilardi House, Tacubaya, Mexico City

1967–68 San Cristobal, Los Clubes, Mexico City

1958–61 Las Arboledas, Mexico City

1957 Satellite City Towers, Queretaro Highway, Mexico City

1955 Capuchinas Sacramentarias del Purismo Corazón de Maria, Chapel and Convent Restoration, Tialpan, Mexico

1954 Antonio Galvez House, San Angel, Mexico City

1952 José Arriola Adame House, Guadalajara, Mexico

1950 House, 130 Avenida de las Fuentes, Mexico City

House, 140 Avenida de las Fuentes, Mexico City

1948 Two Houses, 10/12 Avenida de las Fuentes, Mexico City

1947 Luis Barragan House, Tacubaya, Mexico City

1945–50 Parque Residencial Jardines del Pedregal de San Angel, Mexico City

1944 "El Cabrío" Garden, Mexico City

1940 Ortega House, Mexico City

Arturo Figueroa Uriza houses, Mexico City

1936 Parque México, Mexico City

1929 Franko House, Guadalajara

G. Cristo House, Guadalajara

SELECTED AWARDS

1980 Pritzker Prize for Architecture

Peter Behrens

1868 Born in Hamburg, Germany

1886 Studied painting at the Kunstakademie, Karlsruhe

1890 Continued painting studies in Munich under Hugo Kotschenreiter

1893 Founding member of the Munich Secession

1899 Appointed to the Künstler-Kolonie, Darmstadt

1903 Appointed Director of the Kunstgewerbeschule, Düsseldorf

1907–14 Named Artistic Adviser at AEG (Allgemeine Elektrizitäts-Gesellschaft), Berlin

1922–27 Director of the School of Architecture at the Akademie der Bildenden Künste, Vienna, Austria

1936 Appointed Director of the Architecture Department at the Preussische Akademie der Künste, Berlin

1940 Died in Berlin

SELECTED WORKS

1932 Alexander and Berolina Building, Berlin

1931 Ganz House, Kronberg, Germany

1930 Villa Lewin, Berlin

1927 Weißenhofsiedlung house, Stuttgart, Germany

1925 Good Hope Company, office, stores, and warehouse, Oberhausen, Germany

"New Ways" house for W. J. Basset-Lowke, Northampton, England

1924 IG Farben Dyeworks, Hoechst, Germany

1920 Continental Administration Building, Hannover, Germany

1916 Office/factory building for the Nationale Automobil Aktien-Gesellschaft, Oberschöneweide, Germany

1912 Gas Works, Frankfurt-am-Main, Germany

Wiegand House, Berlin

AEG Railway Equipment Factory, Berlin

1911 Administrative building for the Mannesmann Röhren-Werke, Düsseldorf, Germany

German Embassy, St. Petersburg, Russia

AEG Small Motor Factory, Berlin

1910 "Elektra" Boathouse, Berlin

AEG High Tension Factory, Berlin

1909 AEG Turbine Factory, Berlin

1906 Crematorium, Hagen, Germany

Obenauer House, Saarbrücken

1905 Haus Schede, Wetter an der Ruhr, Germany

1904 Restaurant Jungbrunnen, Exhibition, Düsseldorf, Germany

1902 Hamburg Vestibule ("The Tomb of the Unknown Superman"), Esposizione Internazionale d'Arte Decorative, Turin, Italy

1901 Behrens House, Darmstadt, Germany

Henry N. Cobb

1926 Born in Boston, Massachusetts

1947 Graduated from Harvard College

1949 Master of Architecture, Harvard University Graduate School of Design

1955 One of three founding principals of Pei Cobb Freed & Partners (formerly I.M. Pei & Associates)

SELECTED WORKS

In progress Tour Hines at la Défense, Paris

Friend Center for Engineering Education, Princeton University

Knafel Center for Government and International Studies, Harvard University

1999 College-Conservatory of Music at the University of Cincinnati

China Europe International Business School, Shanghai

Head Office of ABN-AMRO Bank, Amsterdam

World Trade Center, Barcelona, Spain

1996 Headquarters for the American Association for the Advancement of Science, Washington, D. C.

1991 Headquarters of Credit Suisse First Boston at Canary Wharf, London

1987 IBM and Conrail Towers at Commerce Square, Philadelphia, Pennsylvania

1985 Pitney-Bowes World Headquarters, Stamford, Connecticut

1983 Portland Museum of Art, Portland, Maine

1983 World Headquarters of Johnson & Johnson, New Brunswick, New Jersey

1978 ANZ Bank Tower and Regent Hotel at Collins Place, Melbourne, Australia

1976 John Hancock Tower, Boston, Massachusetts

1962 Royal Bank of Canada Building at Place Ville Marie, Montréal, Canada

SELECTED AWARDS

1995 Topaz Medallion for Excellence in Architectural Education, AIA/Association of Collegiate Schools of Architecture

1992 Lifetime Achievement Award, New York Society of Architects

1985 Chicago Architecture Award, Illinois Council of the American Institute of Architects

1982 Medal of Honor, New York Chapter of the American Institute of Architects

1981 Poses Creative Arts Award (Medal for Architecture), Brandeis University

1977 Arnold W. Brunner Memorial Prize, American Academy of Arts and Letters

PROFESSIONAL AFFILIATIONS

Fellow, American Institute of Architects

Fellow, American Academy of Arts and Sciences

Fellow, National Academy of Design

Member of the American Academy of Arts and Letters

Sergei M. Eisenstein

1898 Born in Riga, Latvia (Russian Empire)

1916–18 Studied at the Institute of Civil Engineering, St. Petersburg

1918 Enlisted in the Red Army

1920 Entered the Proletkult Theater (Theater of the People) in Moscow as an assistant decorator

1923 Made a short film, *Glumov's Diary*

1929 Visited Paris, where he filmed *Romance Sentimentale*

1930–32 Worked for Paramount Studios, Hollywood

1932 Went to Mexico, where he filmed *¡Qué Viva México!* (never completed by Eisenstein)

1933 Returned to Moscow

1948 Died in Moscow

FILMOGRAPHY

1958 *Ivan the Terrible* (Part Two)

1944 *Ivan the Terrible* (Part One)

1938 *Alexander Nevsky*

1929 *Old and New* (The General Line)

1928 *October* (Ten Days that Shook the World)

1925 *Potemkin*

1924 *Strike*

Fatehpur Sikri

LOCATION

Uttar Pradesh State, North India. Masterpiece of Moslem architecture.

FOUNDED

1569, by the Mugal Emperor Akbar

DESERTED

1605

NOTABLE BUILDINGS

Buland Darwaza Gate, principal entrance

Jami Masjid, the Great Mosque

Salim Chishti Mausoleum

Jodh Bai Palace

Birbal Palace

Panch Mahal, Royal Audience Hall

Norman Foster

1935 Born in Manchester, England

1961 Graduated from Manchester University School of Architecture and City Planning

1962 Master of Architecture, Yale University School of Architecture

1963 Cofounded (with Richard and Su Rogers and Wendy Cheesman) Team 4 Architects, London

1967 Established Foster and Partners (formerly Foster Associates) in London

1990 Knighted

1999 Made a Life Baron of the United Kingdom

SELECTED WORKS

In progress Swiss Re Headquarters, London

Greater London Authority Headquarters, London

2001 Inner Harbour Masterplan at Duisburg, Germany

Musée de Préhistoire des Gorges de Verdon, Quinson, France

2000 Queen Elizabeth ll Great Court, British Museum

Millennium Bridge, London

1999 New German Parliament, Reichstag, Berlin

1998 Hong Kong International Airport, Hong Kong

Sir Alexander Fleming Building, Medical Research Facility, Imperial College, London

1997 Commerzbank Headquarters, Frankfurt

1995 Faculty of Law, University of Cambridge, England

Bilbao Metro, Bilbao, Spain

1994 Joslyn Art Museum Addition, Omaha, Nebraska

1986 Hong Kong and Shanghai Banking Corporation Headquarters, Hong Kong

1975 Willis Faber and Dumas Offices, Ipswich, Massachusetts

1971 IBM Pilot Head Office, Cosham, England

1966 Reliance Controls Electronics Factory, Swindon, England

SELECTED AWARDS

1999 Pritzker Prize for Architecture

1994 Gold Medal, American Institute of Architects

1992 Arnold W. Brunner Memorial Prize, American Academy of Arts and Letters

1983 Gold Medal, Royal Institute of British Architects

PROFESSIONAL AFFILIATIONS

Member, the Royal Institute of British Architects

Honorary Fellow, American Institute of Architects

Honorary Member, Bund Deutscher Architekten (BDA)

Mario Gandelsonas

1938 Born in Buenos Aires, Argentina

1962 Diploma of Architecture, University of Buenos Aires

1968 Certificate, Centre de Recherches d'Urbanisme, Paris

1972–84 Fellow, Institute for Architecture and Urban Studies, New York

1973 Founding Editor of *Oppositions*

1980 Cofounded Agrest and Gandelsonas Architects, New York

1988 Taught at Yale University School of Architecture

SELECTED WORKS

2000 House in Madrid, Spain

1996 New Town, Shanghai, China

1995 Melrose Community Center, Bronx South, New York

1994 Red Bank Vision Plan, Monmouth County, New Jersey

1992 Hillside Residential Neighborhood, Des Moines, Iowa

Cranbrook Campus Gate, Cranbrook Academy, Bloomfield Hills, Michigan

Vision Plan, Des Moines, Iowa

1990 House on Sagpond, Sagaponack, New York

1988 Duplex on Central Park West, New York

1982 Apartment buildings in Buenos Aires, Argentina

1976 Project for the Les Halles Competition

1975 Roosevelt Island Competition

SELECTED PUBLICATIONS

1999 *X-Urbanism: Architecture and the American City* (Princeton Architectural Press)

1994 *Agrest and Gandelsonas Works* (Princeton Architectural Press)

1992 *The Urban Text: The Chicago Institute of Architecture and Urbanism* (MIT Press)

1972–2001 Numerous articles published in national and international magazines, anthologies, and books

PROFESSIONAL AFFILIATIONS

Professor, Princeton University School of Architecture

Member of the Editorial Board, *Assemblage: A Critical Journal of Architecture and Design Culture* (MIT Press)

Michael Graves

1934 Born in Indianapolis, Indiana

1958 Bachelor of Science, University of Cincinnati

1959 Master of Architecture, Harvard University Graduate School of Design

1964 Established a private practice in Princeton, New Jersey

SELECTED WORKS

1998 NCAA 2000: Headquarters and Hall of Champions, Indianapolis, Indiana

Cincinnati Art Museum Master Plan, Cincinnati, Ohio

Fortis AG Headquarters, Brussels, Belgium

1997 Washington Monument Restoration Scaffolding and Interior Design, Washington, D. C.

1996 United States Courthouse Annex, Washington, D. C.

1995 Post Office, Celebration, Florida

1992 Kasumi Research and Training Center, Tsukuba City, Japan

1990 Central Library, Denver. Colorodo

1990 Emory University Art Museum, Atlanta, Georgia

1986 The Disney Company Corporate Headquarters, Burbank, California

1985–88 Whitney Museum Addition, New York

1983 Humana Corporation Headquarters, Louisville, Kentucky

Public Library, San Juan Capistrano, California

1982 Environmental Education Center, Liberty State Park, Jersey City, New Jersey

Portland Municipal, Portland, Oregon

1978 Fargo-Moorhead Cultural Center, Fargo, North Dakota and Moorhead, Minnesota

1977 Plocek House, Warren, New Jersey

1973 Alexander House, Princeton, New Jersey

1972 Snyderman House, Fort Wayne, Indiana

1969 Benacerraf House Extension, Princeton, New Jersey

1965 Hanselman House, Fort Wayne, Indiana

SELECTED AWARDS

2001 Gold Medal, the American Institute of Architects

1999 National Medal of Arts

1980 Arnold W. Brunner Memorial Prize, American Academy of Arts and Letters

1960–62 Rome Prize Fellow, American Academy in Rome

PROFESSIONAL AFFILIATIONS

Fellow, American Institute of Architects

Member, American Academy of Arts and Letters

Schirmer Professor of Architecture, Princeton University

Vittorio Gregotti

1927 Born in Novara, Italy

1952 Graduated in architecture from the Milan Polytechnic

1974 Founded Gregotti Associati in Milan

1982–96 Editor-in-Chief, *Casabella*

SELECTED WORKS

In progress Guggenheim Museum Venice of Contemporary Art (Punta della Dogana), Venice

Business Center, Abidjan, Ivory Coast

1997 Trussardi Boutique, Place Vendôme, Paris

1995 Accademia Carrara Museum of Modern and Contemporary Art, Carrara, Italy

1994 New Master Plan, Sesto San Giovanni, Milan, Italy

IVI Chemical Research Center, Quattordio, Alessandria, Italy

1993 Cultural Center of Belêm, Lisbon, Portugal

1991 Land Brandenburg regional park, Potsdam, Germany

Sports Palace, Nîmes, France

1988 Olympic Stadium, Barcelona, Spain

ENEA Research Center, Rome, Italy

Office and commercial buildings, Piazzale Kennedy, La Spezia, Italy

1986 Montedison (later ENEA) Research Center, Portici, Naples, Italy

1984–85 Piazza Madrice: Chiesa Madre, Torre Federiciana, Palazzo Comunale, Menfi, Agrigento

1982 General Town Plan, Scandicci, Florence, Italy

1980 IBA residences, Lutzowstraße, Berlin

1973 New campus of the Università degli Studi della Calabria, Cosenza, Italy

ZEN residential district, Palermo, Italy

1972 Facory and offices for the Gabel Textile Company, Rovallasca, Como, Italy

1969–90 New science departments for the Università degli Studi at the Parco d'Orlêans, Palermo, Italy

1960 Office of the Banca Popolare di Novara, Bra, Cuneo, Italy

1956 Workers' housing, Bossi Textile Company, Cameri, Italy

SELECTED WRITINGS

1993 *La città visible* (Einaudi)

1991 *Dentro l'architettura* (Bolate Boringhieri); 1996 English translation: *Inside Architecture* (MIT)

PROFESSIONAL AFFILIATIONS

Member, Accademia di San Luca

Member, Accademia di Brera

Member, Bund der Deutschen Architekten (BDA)

Honorary member, the American Institute of Architects

Charles Gwathmey

1938 Born in Charlotte, North Carolina

1959 Bachelor of Architecture, University of Pennsylvania

1962 Master of Architecture, Yale University School of Architecture

1968 Cofounded Gwathmey Siegel & Associates, New York

SELECTED WORKS

2000 Tangeman University Center, University of Cincinnati, Ohio

1998 United States Mission to the United Nations, New York

1997 Basketball Hall of Fame, Springfield, Massachusetts

1996 The David Geffen Building, Beverly Hills, California

1993 Levitt Center for University Advancement, University of Iowa, Iowa City, Iowa

1992 Henry Art Gallery Renovation and Addition, University of Washington, Seattle

1991 The Science, Industry and Business Library (New York Public Library), New York

1990 Zumikon Residence, Zumikon, Switzerland

1988 Werner Otto Hall, Busch-Reisinger Museum/Fine Arts Library (Addition to the Fogg Museum), Harvard University

1985 Morgan Stanley Dean Witter & Co. World Headquarters, New York

1982 Solomon R. Guggenheim Museum Renovation and Addition, New York

1979 de Menil Residence, East Hampton, New York

1970 Whig Hall Renovation, Princeton University, Princeton, New Jersey

1965 Gwathmey Residence and Studio, Amagansett, New York

SELECTED AWARDS

1990 New York State Society of Architects Lifetime Achievement Award

1988 Guild Hall Academy of Arts Lifetime Achievement Medal in Visual Arts

1985 Yale Alumni Arts Award, Yale University School of Architecture

1983 Medal of Honor, American Institute of Architects New York Chapter

1982 Firm Award (Gwathmey Siegel & Associates Architects), American Institute of Architects

1970 Arnold W. Brunner Memorial Prize, American Academy of Arts and Letters

1962–63 Fulbright Fellowship (France)

PROFESSIONAL AFFILIATIONS

Fellow, American Institute of Architects

Member, American Academy of Arts and Letters

Trustee, the Cooper Union for the Advancement of Science and Art

Hugh Hardy

1932 Born in Majorca, Spain

1954 Graduated from Princeton University

1956 Master of Architecture, Princeton University School of Architecture

1956–58 Served in the Army Corps of Engineers

1958–62 Worked with Eero Saarinen and Jo Mielziner on construction of the Vivian Beaumont Theater at Lincoln Center

1962 Established Hugh Hardy & Associates

1967 Cofounded Hardy Holzman Pfeiffer Associates in New York

SELECTED WORKS

2000 Bridgemarket, New York

Brasserie 82, New York

1999 Radio City Music Hall Restoration, New York

1998 BAM Café and BAM Rose Cinemas, Brooklyn Academy of Music, Brooklyn, New York

1996 Windows on the World, World Trade Center, New York

U.S. Customs and Immigration Center at Rainbow Bridge, Niagara Falls, New York

1993 Los Angeles Central Library, Los Angeles, California

Scholastic Inc. Headquarters, New York

1992 Bryant Park and Bryant Park Grill, New York

1990 New Haven Free Public Library Renovation and Expansion, New Haven, Connecticut

1988 Alaska Center for the Performing Arts, Anchorage, Alaska

1987 Brooklyn Academy of Music Majestic Theatre Renovation, Brooklyn, New York

1986 Robert O. Anderson Building, Los Angeles County Museum of Art, Los Angeles, California

1982 Joyce Theater Renovation, New York

1977 Brooklyn Children's Museum, Brooklyn, New York

Sculpture Hall and East Wing, St. Louis Art Museum, St. Louis, Missouri

1976 Cooper-Hewitt National Design Museum (adaptive reuse), New York

1974 Columbus Occupational Health Center, Columbus, Ohio

1968 Playhouse in the Park, Cincinnati, Ohio

SELECTED AWARDS

1999 Governor's Arts Award, New York State Council on the Arts

1981 Firm Award (Hardy Holzman Pfeiffer Associates), American Institute of Architects

1978 Medal of Honor (Hardy Holzman Pfeiffer Associates), American Institute of Architects New York Chapter

1974 Arnold W. Brunner Memorial Prize (Hardy Holzman Pfeiffer Associates), American Academy of Arts and Letters

PROFESSIONAL AFFILIATIONS

Fellow, American Institute of Architects

Fellow, National Academy of Design

Arata Isozaki

1931 Born in Oita, Japan

1954 Graduated from the University of Tokyo

1963 Established a private practice, Oita

SELECTED WORKS

1998 Akiyoshidai International Arts Village, Yamaguchi, Japan

Higashi Shizuoka Cultural Complex Project, Shizuoka, Japan

1998 Nara Centennial Hall, Nara, Japan

1995 DOMUS: La Casa del Hombre, La Coruña, Spain

1994 Kyoto Concert Hall, Kyoto, Japan

The Center of Japanese Art and Technology, Krakow, Poland

1990 Team Disney building, Buena Vista, Florida

Sant Jordi Sports Palace, Barcelona, Spain

Art Tower Mito, Ibaragi, Japan

1989 Kashi Twin Towers, Fukuoka, Japan

1986 Museum of Contemporary Art (MOCA), Los Angeles, California

1979 Space & Time in Japan "MA," Exhibition Festival D'Autonne, Paris, France

1974 Museum of Modern Art, Gunma, Japan

1970 Expo '70 Festival Plaza, Osaka, Japan

1966 Oita Prefectural Library, Oita, Japan

SELECTED AWARDS

1992 Honor Award, American Institute of Architects

1988 Arnold W. Brunner Memorial Prize, American Academy of Arts and Letters

1986 Gold Medal, Royal Institute of British Architects

PROFESSIONAL AFFILIATIONS

Honorary Fellow, Royal Academy of Arts, Honorary Academician, England

Honorary Fellow, American Institute of Architects

Honorary Fellow, Royal Institute of British Architects (RIBA)

Honorary Fellow, Bund Deutscher Architekten (BDA)

Carlos Jimenez

1959 Born in San José, Costa Rica

1981 Bachelor of Architecture, University of Houston College of Architecture

1982 Established Carlos Jimenez Studio, Houston, Texas

SELECTED WORKS

2001 DePauw University Art Center, Greencastle, Indiana

2000 Cummins Child Development Center, Columbus, Indiana

Whatley Library, Austin, Texas

1996 Spencer Studio Art Building, Williams College, Williamstown, Massachusetts

1994 Central Administration Junior School Building,
Museum of Fine Arts, Houston, Texas

1994 Wilson House, Brooks County, Texas

1992 Saito House, Houston, Texas

1990 Lynn Goode Gallery, Houston, Texas

Chadwick House, Houston, Texas

1989 Beauchamp House, Houston, Texas

1986 Houston Fine Art Press, Houston, Texas

1983 Jimenez House and Studio, Houston, Texas

SELECTED AWARDS

1995 Forty Under Forty Award, New York

1994 Emerging Voices Award, Architectural League of New York

1988 Young Architects Award, Architectural League of New York

1987 Young Architects Award, *Progressive Architecture*

Sumet Jumsai

1939 Born in Bangkok, Thailand

1950–57 Educated in Paris and in England

1958 Matriculated at Cambridge University, England

1967 Ph.D., Architecture, Cambridge University, England

1969 Established SJA+3D (formerly Sumet Jumsai Associates)
in Bangkok, Thailand

SELECTED WORKS

1999 Hotel Plaza Athenee, Bangkok, Thailand

1995 Nation Tower, Bangkok East, Thailand

1993 Grand Pacific Hotel, Bangkok, Thailand

1992 International School of Bangkok, Thailand

1991 Nation Building, Bangkok East, Thailand

1986–99 Thammasat University, Rangsit Campus, Bangkok North, Thailand

1986 Robot Building (Bank of Asia Headquarters), Bangkok, Thailand

1976 Science Museum, Bangkok, Thailand

1970 British Council Building, Bangkok, Thailand

SELECTED AWARDS

1999 Crystal Award for Art and Culture, World Economic Forum

1998 Thailand's National Artist (architectural category)

1982–91 Nine Gold Medal Awards of the Association of Siamese Architects under Royal Patronage

PROFESSIONAL AFFILIATIONS

Honorary Fellow, American Institute of Architects

Faculty, Department of Architecture, Cambridge University

Louis I. Kahn

1901 Born in Ösel Island, Russia (now Saaremaa Island, Estonia)

1924 Bachelor of Architecture, University of Pennsylvania

1928–29 European tour

1935 Established a practice with Alfred Kastner

1941 Formed a partnership with George Howe

1947–57 Design critic and professor at the Yale University School of Architecture

1957 Named the Paul Philippe Cret Professor of Architecture at the University of Pennsylvania

1974 Died in New York

SELECTED WORKS

1974 Yale Center for British Art, New Haven

Institute of Management, Ahmedabad, India

Sher-e-Bangla Nagar, Capital of Bangladesh, Dhaka, Bangladesh

1972 Kimbell Art Museum, Fort Worth, Texas

Library and Dining Hall, Phillips Exeter Academy, Exeter, New Hampshire

Temple Beth-El Synagogue, Chappaqua, New York

1970 Olivetti-Underwood Factory, Harrisburg, Pennsylvania

1969 First Unitarian Church and School, Rochester, New York

1965 Eleanor Donnelly Erdman Hall, Bryn Mawr College, Bryn Mawr, Pennsylvania

Salk Institute for Biological Studies, La Jolla, California

1961 Richards Medical Research Laboratories, University of Pennsylvania, Philadelphia

1960 Norman Fisher House, Philadelphia

1956 Jewish Community Center, Trenton, New Jersey

1953 Yale University Art Gallery, New Haven, Connecticut

SELECTED AWARDS

1972 Gold Medal, Royal Institute of British Architects

1971 Gold Medal, American Institute of Architects

1970 Medal of Honor, American Institute of Architects New York Chapter

1965 Medal of Honor, Danish Architectural Association

1960 Arnold W. Brunner Memorial Prize, American Academy of Arts and Letters

1950 Rome Prize Fellow, American Academy in Rome

PROFESSIONAL AFFILIATIONS

Fellow, American Institute of Architects

Fellow, American Academy of Arts and Sciences

Member of the American Academy of Arts and Letters

Le Corbusier

1887 Born Charles-Edouard Jeanneret in La Chaux-de-Fonds, Switzerland

1900 Matriculated at l'École d'Art, La Chaux-de-Fonds, where Charles L'Eplattenier's influence was formative

1909 Worked for Auguste and Gustave Perret, Paris

1910 Worked for Peter Behrens, Berlin

1917 Established a private practice, Paris

1919 Founding Editor of *L'Esprit Nouveau*

1927 League of Nations competition

1928 Played a leading role in the creation of the Congrès Internationaux d'Architecture Moderne (CIAM)

1965 Died in Roquebrune-Cap-Martin (Alpes-Maritimes), France

SELECTED WORKS

1962 Carpenter Center for the Visual Arts, Harvard University, Cambridge, Massachusetts

1960 National Museum of Western Art, Tokyo, Japan

1956–64 Capitol Buildings, Chandigarh, India

1954 Millowners' Association Headquarters, Ahmadabad, India

Convent Sainte-Marie de la Tourette, Eveux, France

1953 United Nations Headquarters (with Wallace Harrison et al.), New York

1951 Chapelle Nôtre Dame du Haut, Ronchamp, France

1947 Unité d'Habitation, Marseille, France

1936 Ministry of Education and Health, Rio de Janeiro, Brazil

1932 Palais du Peuple (Salvation Army), Paris, France

1930 Swiss Pavilion, Cité Universitaire, Paris, France

1928 Savoye House, Poissy, France

1927 Weißenhof houses, Stuttgart, Germany

Stein House, Garches, France

1923 La Roche House, Paris, France

1922 Ozenfant house and studio, Paris, France

1916 Villa Schwob, La Chaux-de-Fonds, France

1912 Jeanneret-Perret and Favre-Jacot Houses, La Chaux-de-Fonds, France

SELECTED PUBLICATIONS

1950 *Le Modulor*

1937 *Quand les cathédrales étaient blanches*

1935 *La Ville radieuse*

1925 *Urbanisme*

1923 *Vers une architecture*

Ricardo Legorreta

1931 Born in Mexico City

1952 Bachelor of Architecture, Universidad Nacional Autónoma de México (UNAM)

1948–55 Draftsman and Project Manager for José Villagrán

1955–60 Partnership with José Villagrán

1963 Established Legorreta & Legorreta (formerly Legorreta Arquitectos) in Mexico City

1977 Founded LA Designs, a firm specializing in furniture and accessories

1985 Founded Legorreta Arquitectos, USA

SELECTED WORKS

In progress Mexican Museum, San Francisco

Sheraton Bilbao, Spain

2001 Max Palevsky Residential Commons, University of Chicago

2000 Escuela de Graduados en Administración y Dirección de Empresas (EGADE), Mexico City

Mexican Pavilion at Expo Hanover 2000, Germany

1999 College of Santa Fe Visual Arts Center, Santa Fe, Mexico

1997 Schwab Residential Center, Stanford University School of Business, Palo Alto, California

Tech Museum of Innovation, San Jose, California

1995 San Antonio Central Library, San Antonio, Texas

1994 Pershing Square, Los Angeles, California

Monterrey Central Library, Monterrey, Nuevo León, Mexico

Metropolitan Cathedral, Managua, Nicaragua

1993 Papalote Museo del Niño, Mexico City

Plaza Reforma Corporate Center, Mexico City

1991 Monterrey Museum of Contemporary Art (MARCO), Monterrey, Nuevo León, Mexico

1988–90 Solana IBM Campus, Dallas, Texas

1985 Renault Factory, Durango, Mexico

1981 Camino Real Hotel, Ixtapa, Mexico

1968 Camino Real Hotel, Mexico City

SELECTED AWARDS

2000 Gold Medal, American Institute of Architects

1999 Gold Medal, Union Internationale des Architectes (UIA)

1991 Fine Arts National Award, Mexican Government

PROFESSIONAL AFFILIATIONS

Honorary Fellow, Society of Mexican Architects

Honorary Fellow, American Institute of Architects

Honorary Fellow, Royal Institute of British Architects

Member, American Academy of Arts and Sciences

William S. W. Lim

1932 Born in Hong Kong

1955 Graduated from the Architectural Association, London

1956–57 Fulbright Fellow, Harvard University Graduate School of Design

1980 Founded William Lim Associates, Singapore

SELECTED WORKS

In progress Experimental Bungalows, Cluny Hill, Singapore

2001 Experimental Bungalows, Jalan Haji Alias, Singapore

2000 Gallery Evason Hotel, Singapore

Marine Parade Community Club and Regional Library, Singapore

1995 Cahaya House, Malaysia

1992–94 LaSalle College of the Arts, Singapore

1990 Reuter House, Singapore

Central Square, Kuala Lumpur, Malaysia

1989 Tampines Community Center, Singapore

1984 House at Emerald Hill Road, Singapore

Unit 8 Condominium, Singapore

1980 Chapel of the Resurrection, Singapore

1979 Thai House, Singapore

1978 St. Andrew's Junior College, Singapore

1974 Golden Mile Complex, Singapore

1973 People's Park Complex, Singapore

1965 NTUC Conference Hall, Singapore

SELECTED AWARDS

1956 Fulbright Fellowship

PROFESSIONAL AFFILIATIONS

Founding Member, Singapore Heritage Society

Founder and President, AA Asia

Adjunct Professor, Royal Melbourne Institute of Technology

Guest Professor, Tianjin University, China

Maison de Verre

ARCHITECTS
Pierre Chareau and Bernard Bijvoet

BUILT 1927–32

LOCATION
Paris

TYPE Residential; early modern interior inserted into existing structure

MATERIALS
Steel, glass, glass block

Richard Meier

1934 Born in Newark, New Jersey

1957 Bachelor of Architecture, Cornell University

1963 Founded Richard Meier & Partners, New York

SELECTED WORKS

2000 Church of the Year, Rome

United States Courthouse and Federal Building, Central Islip, New York

1997 The Getty Center, Los Angeles

1995 City Hall and Central Library, The Hague

Swissair North American Headquarters, Melville, New York

Museum of Contemporary Art, Barcelona, Spain

1993 Hypolux Bank Building, Luxembourg

Exhibition and Assembly Building, Ulm, Germany

Daimler-Benz Research Center, Ulm, Germany

1992 Canal+ Headquarters, Paris

Weishaupt Forum, Schwendi, Germany

1985–89 Grotta House, Harding Township, New Jersey

1985 Museum for Decorative Arts, Frankfurt am Main, Germany

1983 High Museum of Art, Atlanta, Georgia

1981 Hartford Seminary, Hartford, Connecticut

1979 The Atheneum, New Harmony, Indiana

1977 Bronx Development Center, Bronx, New York

1967 Smith House, Darien, Connecticut

SELECTED AWARDS

1997 Præmium Imperiale

Gold Medal, American Institute of Architects

1989 Royal Gold Medal, Royal Institute of British Architects

1984 Pritzker Prize for Architecture

1980 Medal of Honor, American Institute of Architects New York Chapter

1973 Rome Prize Fellow, American Academy in Rome

1972 Arnold W. Brunner Memorial Prize, American Academy of Arts and Letters

PROFESSIONAL AFFILIATIONS

Fellow, American Institute of Architects

Fellow, National Academy of Design

Fellow, American Academy of Arts and Sciences

Member, American Academy of Arts and Letters

William Pedersen

1938 Born in St. Paul, Minnesota

1961 Bachelor of Architecture, University of Minnesota

1963 Master of Architecture, Massachusetts Institute of Technology

1976 Cofounded Kohn Pedersen Fox Associates in New York

Principal and Partner-in-Charge of Design, Kohn Pedersen Fox Associates

SELECTED WORKS

In progress U.S. Air International Terminal, Philadelphia

Jon M. Huntsman Hall, Wharton School of Business, University of Pennsylvania, Philadelphia

Gannett/USA TODAY Headquarters, Tysons Corner, Virginia

Posteel Headquarters, Seoul, Korea

Shanghai World Financial Center, Shanghai, China

2001 Baruch College Academic Complex, City College of New York

1997 IBM World Headquarters, Armonk, New York

Greater Buffalo International Airport

The World Bank, Washington, D. C.

1996 First Hawaiian Bank, Honolulu, Hawaii

1993 United States Embassy, Nicosia, Cyprus

Westendstraße 1/DG Bank Headquarters, Germany

1992 Federal Reserve Bank, Dallas, Texas

IBM Quebec Headquarters, Montreal, Canada

1991 The St. Paul Companies Headquarters, St. Paul, Minnesota

Goldman Sachs European Headquarters, London

1985 Procter & Gamble General Offices Complex, Cincinnati, Ohio

1983 333 Wacker Drive, Chicago, Illinois

SELECTED AWARDS

1998 Gold Medal, Tau Sigma Delta (National Architectural Honor Society)

1990 Firm Award (KPF), American Institute of Architects

University of Minnesota Alumni Achievement Award

1989 Medal of Honor (KPF), American Institute of Architects New York Chapter

1985 Arnold W. Brunner Memorial Prize, American Academy of Arts and Letters

1965 The Rome Prize in Architecture, American Academy in Rome

PROFESSIONAL AFFILIATIONS

Fellow, American Institute of Architects

Fellow, American Academy in Rome

Cesar Pelli

1926 Born in Tucumán, Argentina

1949 Graduated in architecture from Universidad Nacional de Tucumán

1954 Master of Architecture, University of Illinois

1954–64 Designer at Eero Saarinen & Associates, Bloomfield Hills, Michigan

1964–68 Director of Design at Daniel, Mann, Johnson & Mendenhall, Los Angeles, California

1968–76 Partner for Design at Gruen Associates, Los Angeles

1977 Established Cesar Pelli & Associates in New Haven, Connecticut

1977–84 Dean of the Yale School of Architecture

SELECTED WORKS

1997 Bank of Boston Tower, Buenos Aires, Argentina

North Terminal, Washington National Airport, Washington, D. C.

1996 Chubu Cultural Center, Kurayoshi, Japan

1995 National Museum of Contemporary Art, Osaka, Japan

U.S. Federal Courthouse Building, Brooklyn, New York

1994 Owens Corning World Headquarters, Toledo, Ohio

1991 Aranoff Center for the Arts, Cincinnati, Ohio

Canary Wharf Tower, London, England

1990 NTT Headquarters, Tokyo

1987 Carnegie Hall Tower, New York

1985 Norwest Corporate Center, Minneapolis, Minnesota

1984 Herring Hall, Rice University, Texas

1977 Museum of Modern Art Expansion and Renovation, New York City

1975 Winter Garden, Niagara Falls, New York

1972 U. S. Embassy, Tokyo, Japan

SELECTED AWARDS

1995 Gold Medal, American Institute of Architects

1993 Won international design competition for Abandoibarra Master Plan, Bilbao, Spain

1991 Won international design competition for Petronas Towers, Kuala Lumpur, Malaysia

1989 Firm Award, American Institute of Architects

1984 Won international design competition for World Financial Center, New York

1978 Arnold W. Brunner Memorial Prize, American Academy of Arts and Letters

PROFESSIONAL AFFILIATIONS

Fellow, American Institute of Architects (AIA)

Fellow, American Academy of Arts and Sciences

Academician, American Academy of Arts and Letters

Member, National Academy of Design

Academician, International Academy of Architecture

Member, L'Academie d'Architecture de France

Member, Russian Academy of Architecture and Construction Services

Honorary Member, Sociedad de Arquitectos de Cordoba

James Stewart Polshek

1930 Born in Akron, Ohio

1951 Bachelor of Science, Western Reserve University

1955 Master of Architecture, Yale University School of Architecture

1963 Founded Polshek Partnership Architects (formerly Polshek & Partners) in New York

1972–87 Dean of the Columbia University Graduate School of Architecture, Planning and Preservation

SELECTED WORKS

In progress William J. Clinton Presidential Center, Little Rock, Arkansas

Newseum and Freedom Forum International Headquarters, Washington, D. C.

Yale University Art Gallery Renovation and Expansion, New Haven, Connecticut

Brooklyn Museum of Art, Plaza and Entry Pavilion, Brooklyn, New York

2001 Carnegie Hall, Zankel Hall, New York City

COPIA: The American Center for Wine, Food, and the Arts, Napa, California

2000 Rose Center for Earth and Space, American Museum of Natural History, New York City

Scandinavia House, New York City

1998 Mashantucket Pequot Museum and Research Center, Mashantucket, Connecticut

Santa Fe Opera Theater, Santa Fe, New Mexico

1997 *The New York Times* Printing Plant, Queens, New York

1995 Inventure Place, Home of the National Inventors Hall of Fame, Akron, Ohio

1993 Center for the Arts Theater, Yerba Buena Gardens, San Francisco, California

1992 Brooklyn Museum of Art Renovation and Expansion, Phase II, Brooklyn, New York

1991 Seamen's Church Institute, New York

1987 Carnegie Hall restoration and renovation, New York City

1980 500 Park Tower, New York City

1972 New York State Bar Center, Albany, New York

1963 Tejin Institute for Biomedical Research, Tokyo, Japan

SELECTED AWARDS

1992 Firm Award (Polshek Partnership), American Institute of Architects

1986 Medal of Honor (Polshek Partnership), American Institute of Architects, New York Chapter

1956–57 Fulbright Fellowship, Royal Academy of Fine Arts, Copenhagen, Denmark

PROFESSIONAL AFFILIATIONS

Fellow, American Institute of Architects

Fellow, National Academy of Design

Founder and Member, Board of Advisors of Architects, Designers and Planners for Social Responsibility

Founder and Member, Board of Directors of the Temple Hoyne Buell Center for the Study of American Architecture

Antoine Predock

1936 Born in Lebanon, Missouri

1962 Bachelor of Architecture, Columbia University

1967 Founded Antoine Predock Architect in Albuquerque, New Mexico

SELECTED WORKS

In progress Austin City Hall, Austin, Texas

San Diego Padres Ballpark, San Diego, California

Recreation Center and Competition Natatorium, Ohio State University, Columbus, Ohio

Tacoma Art Museum, Tacoma, Washington

2000 Tang Teaching Museum and Art Gallery, Skidmore College, Saratoga Springs, New York

McNamara Alumni Center/University of Minnesota Gateway, Minneapolis, Minnesota

1997 Spencer Theater for the Performing Arts, Alto, New Mexico

Arizona Science Center, Phoenix, Arizona

1996 Center for Integrated Systems, Stanford University, Palo Alto, California

1995 Museum of Science and Industry, Tampa, Florida

1994 Thousand Oaks Civic Arts Plaza, Thousand Oaks, California

1993 American Heritage Center and Art Museum, University of Wyoming, Laramie, Wyoming

1992 Hotel Santa Fe, Euro Disney, Paris

1989 Nelson Fine Arts Center, Arizona State University, Tempe, Arizona

1967–74 La Luz Community, Albuquerque, New Mexico

SELECTED AWARDS

2000 AIA Western International Gold Medal Distinguished Award of Honor

1999 American Architecture Awards, 1999

1992 Chicago Architecture Award, Illinois Council of the American Institute of Architects

1990 AIA/Western Mountain Region Firm Award

1989 Gran Premio Internacional de la Biennial International de Arquitectura de Buenos Aires

1985 Rome Prize Fellow, American Academy in Rome

PROFESSIONAL AFFILIATIONS

Fellow, American Institute of Architects

Raj Rewal

1934 Born in Punjab, India

1962 Diploma in Architecture, Royal Institute of British Architects, London

1963 Established Raj Rewal Associates in New Delhi

1963–72 Professor at School of Planning and Architecture, New Delhi

1985 Commissioner for the Exhibition on Traditional Architecture of India, Paris

SELECTED WORKS

2000 Library for the Indian Parliament, New Delhi

1999 Lisbon Ismaili Centre, Lisbon, Portugal

1996 Housing for British High Commission, New Delhi

1995 World Bank Resident Mission, New Delhi

1990 National Institute of Immunology, New Delhi

1989 SCOPE Office Complex, New Delhi

1983 Central Institute of Education Technology (CIET), New Delhi

1982 Asian Games Olympic Village, New Delhi

1974 550 housing units at Sheikh Sarai, New Delhi

Permanent Exhibition Complex, New Delhi

1969 Nehru Pavilion at Pragati Maidan, New Delhi

French Embassy, Staff quarters, New Delhi

SELECTED AWARDS

1995 Great Masters Award by JK Trust, India

1994 Architect of the Year Award by JK Trust, India

1993 Award, Mexican Association of Architects

1989 Robert Matthew Award by Commonwealth Association of Architects, London

1989 Gold Medal, Indian Institute of Architects

PROFESSIONAL AFFILIATIONS

Associate, Royal Institute of Architects

Fellow, Indian Institute of Architects

H. H. Richardson

1838 Born in St. James Parish, Louisiana

1859 Graduated from Harvard College

1859–60 Studied at l'École des Beaux-Arts, Paris

1866 Established a private practice, New York

1867 Formed a partnership with Charles Dexter Gambrill

1886 Died in Brookline, Massachusetts

SELECTED WORKS

1887 Glessner House, Chicago, Illinois

Allegheny Courthouse and Jail, Pittsburgh, Pennsylvania

Marshall Field Wholesale Store, Chicago, Illinois (demolished 1930)

1885 Henry Adams House, Washington, D. C. (demolished 1927)

John Hay House, Washington, D. C. (demolished 1927)

1884 Austin Hall, Harvard University, Cambridge, Massachusetts

Immanuel Baptist Church, Newton, Massachusetts

1883 M. F. Stoughton House, Cambridge, Massachusetts

1882 Crane Memorial Library, Quincy, Massachusetts

City Hall, Albany, New York

1881 Boston and Albany Railroad Station, Auburndale, Massachusetts

Ames Gate Lodge, North Easton, Massachusetts

1880 Sever Hall, Harvard University, Cambridge, Massachusetts

Dr. James Bryant House, Cohasset, Massachusetts

1879 Ames Free Library, North Easton, Massachusetts

1878 Buffalo State Hospital, Buffalo, New York

Winn Memorial Library, Woburn, Massachusetts

1877 Trinity Church, Boston, Massachusetts

1876 Cheney Building, Hartford, Connecticut

1875 New York State Capitol, Albany, New York

1874 W. W. Sherman House, Newport, Rhode Island

1873 Brattle Square Church, Boston, Massachusetts

1872 F. W. Andrews House, Middletown, Rhode Island (demolished 1920)

1871 William Dorsheimer House, Buffalo, New York

1869 Western Railroad Offices (demolished 1926)

Grace Church, Medford, Massachusetts

Unity Church, Springfield, Massachusetts (demolished 1961)

Rockefeller Center

ARCHITECTS
Reinhard & Hofmeister; Corbett, Harrison & MacMurray; Raymond Hood, Godley & Fouilhoux

BUILT 1931–40

LOCATION
New York

TYPE Skyscraper

MATERIALS
Limestone, aluminum, glass

Richard Rogers

1933 Born in Florence, Italy

1959 Graduated from the Architectural Association, London

1962 Master of Architecture, Yale University School of Architecture (Fulbright Scholar)

1962 Established (with Su Rogers and Norman and Wendy Foster) Team 4 Architects, London

1970 Formed a partnership with Renzo Piano, London

1977 Founded Richard Rogers Partnership, London

1991 Knighted

1996 Made a Life Baron of the United Kingdom

SELECTED WORKS

2000 Lloyd's Register of Shipping, London

Montevetro Building, London

1999 New Millennium Experience/Greenwich Peninsula Masterplan, London

Amano Pharmaceutical Research Laboratories, Gifu, Japan

88 Wood Street Office Development, London

Daimler Chrysler Offices and Housing, Berlin

1998 VR Techno Centre, Gifu, Japan

Tribunal de Grande Instance, Bordeaux, France

1995 European Court of Human Rights, Strasbourg, Germany

1994 Channel 4 Television Headquarters, London

1986 Lloyd's of London Building, London

1983 PA Technology Laboratory, Princeton, New Jersey

1982 Inmos Microprocessor Factory, Newport, South Wales, UK

1981 Fleetguard Manufacturing and Distribution Center, Quimper, France

1977 Centre Pompidou (Beaubourg), Paris

1964 Creek Vean House, Cornwall, UK

SELECTED AWARDS

2000 Præmium Imperiale

1989 Arnold W. Brunner Memorial Prize, American Academy of Arts and Letters

1986 Chevalier, l'Ordre National de la Légion d'Honneur

1985 The Royal Gold Medal for Architecture

PROFESSIONAL AFFILIATIONS

Honorary Fellow, American Institute of Architects

Chair, Government Urban Task Force

Paul Rudolph

1918 Born in Elkton, Kentucky

1940 Bachelor of Architecture, Alabama Polytechnic Institute

1947 Master of Architecture, Harvard Graduate School of Design

1948–52 Established a private practice with Ralph Twitchell in Sarasota, Florida

1952 Started a solo practice in Sarasota, Florida

1958–65 Chairman, Yale University School of Architecture

1965 Established Paul Rudolph, Architect in New York

1997 Died in New York

SELECTED WORKS

1988 Lippo (formerly Bond) Center, Hong Kong, China

1984 City Center Tower, Fort Worth, Texas

1980 William R. Cannon Chapel, Candler School of Theology, Emory University, Atlanta, Georgia

1975 Earl Brydges Memorial Library, Niagara Falls, New York

1972 Waterfront Development Complex, Buffalo, New York

1969 Burroughs Wellcome Corporate Headquarters, Durham, North Carolina

1966 Crawford Manor Housing, New Haven, Connecticut

1964 Endo Laboratories, Garden City, New York

1963 Boston Government Service Center, Boston, Massachusetts

Art and Architecture Building, Yale University, New Haven, Connecticut

Core buildings, Southeastern Massachusetts University, North Dartmouth, Massachusetts

1962 Temple Street Parking Garage, New Haven, Connecticut

1961 Married Student Housing, Yale University, New Haven, Connecticut

1959 William B. Greeley Memorial Laboratory, School of Forestry & Environmental Studies, Yale University, New Haven, Connecticut

Sarasota High School, Sarasota, Florida

1958 Jewett Arts Center, Wellesley College, Wellesley, Massachusetts

1952 Walker Guest House, Sanibel Island, Florida

1951 Wheelan House, Siesta Key, Florida

Cocoon House (Healy Guest House), Siesta Key, Florida

PROFESSIONAL AFFILIATIONS

Fellow, American Institute of Architects

Fellow, American Society of Interior Designers

Eero Saarinen

1910 Born in Kirkkonummi, Finland to noted architect Eliel Saarinen and sculptor Loja Gesellius

1934 Graduated from Yale College, New Haven, Connecticut

1938 Joined Eliel Saarinen's practice in Bloomfield Hills, Michigan

1961 Died in Ann Arbor, Michigan

SELECTED WORKS

1966 Gateway Arch, St. Louis, Missouri

1964 North Christian Church, Columbus, Indiana

CBS Headquarters, New York

1963 John Deere and Company, Moline, Illinois

1962 Dulles International Airport, Chantilly, Virginia

Ezra Stiles and Samuel Morse Colleges, Yale University, New Haven, Connecticut

Trans World Airlines (TWA) Terminal, New York

1960 University of Chicago Law School, Chicago, Illinois

American Embassy, London

1958 David S. Ingalls Hockey Rink, Yale University, New Haven, Connecticut

1957 General Motors Research and Development Center, Warren, Michigan

1955 Kresge Chapel and Auditorium, Massachusetts Institute of Technology, Cambridge, Massachusetts

1954 Irwin Union Bank and Trust Company, Columbus, Indiana

1950 Bell Laboratories, Holmdell, New Jersey

1949 General Motors Technical Center, Warren, Michigan

SELECTED AWARDS

1962 Gold Medal, American Institute of Architects (posthumous)

PROFESSIONAL AFFILIATIONS

Fellow, American Institute of Architects

Der Scutt

1934 Born in Reading, Pennsylvania

1958 Graduated from Pennsylvania State University

1961 Master of Architecture, Yale University School of Architecture

1961–65 Worked for Paul Rudolph, Architect

1965–75 Senior Designer/Associate at Kahn and Jacobs Architects, New York

1975 81 Partner, Swanke Hayden Connell Architects, New York

1981 Established Der Scutt Architect, New York

SELECTED WORKS

2001 Trump–General Motors Building Lobby Renovation, New York

1997–2001 Bankers Trust/Deutsche Bank Interiors, New York

1998 Reading Public Museum Renovation and Expansion, Reading, Pennsylvania

1997 40 Wall Street (Trump Building) Renovation, New York

1995 555 Fifth Avenue Office Building, New York

International Flavors & Fragrances Corporate Headquarters, New York

1989 575 Lexington Avenue Office Tower, New York

International Flavors & Fragrances, Household Products Headquarters, Haglet, New Jersey

Roure Dupont (now Givaudan Roure) Headquarters, New Jersey

1988 625 Madison Avenue Office Tower, New Jersey

The Corinthian (56-story condominium complex), New York City

1985 The Hongkong and Shanghai Bank (HSBC) Headquarters, New York

1984 100 United Nations Plaza (55-Story Condominium Complex), New York City

1982 Trump Tower, New York City

1981 520 Madison Avenue Office Tower, New York City

1980 Grand Hyatt Hotel, New York City

1979 Northwestern Mutual Life Heaqdquarters, Milwaukee, Wisconsin

1974 Hercules Data Center, Delaware

1973 Equitable Life Assurance Data Center, Pennsylvania

One Astor Plaza Office Tower & Legitimate Theatre, New York City

1972 Continental Insurance Corporation Headquarters, New York City

1964 Barlow School Library, Amenia, New York

PROFESSIONAL AFFILIATIONS

Fellow, American Institute of Architects

Robert A. M. Stern

1939 Born in New York

1960 Graduated from Columbia College, New York

1965 Master of Architecture, Yale University School of Architecture

1969–77 Established a partnership with John S. Hagmann, New York

1977 Founded Robert A. M. Stern Architects, New York

1984–88 Director, Temple Hoyne Buell Center for the Study of American Architecture, Columbia University

1998 Appointed Dean of the Yale University School of Architecture

SELECTED WORKS

In progress Hobby Center for the Performing Arts, Houston, Texas

2001 Arts, Media & Communication Building, California State University, Northridge, California

2000 Broadway Residence Hall, Columbia University, New York City

1999 Robert C. Byrd United States Courthouse and Federal Building, Beckley, West Virginia

Smith Campus Center, Pomona College, Claremont, California

1996 William Gates Computer Science Building, Stanford University, Palo Alto, California

1995 Town Plan, Celebration, Florida

1993 42nd Street Now! Master Plan, New York

Roger Tory Peterson Institute, Jamestown, New York

Norman Rockwell Museum, Stockbridge, Massachusetts

1992 Hotel Cheyenne, Euro Disney, Marne-la-Vallée, France

Newport Bay Club, Euro Disney, Marne-la-Vallée, France

1991 Ohrstrom Library, St. Paul's School, Concord, New Hampshire

1985 World Headquarters, Mexx International, Voorschoten, Netherlands

Prospect Point, La Jolla, California

Point West Place office building, Framingham, Massachusetts

1974 Lang House, Washington, Connecticut

Poolhouse, Greenwich, Connecticut

1967 Wiseman House, Montauk, New York

SELECTED AWARDS

1999 Guild Hall Academy of Arts Lifetime Achievement Medal in Visual Arts

1984 Medal of Honor, American Institute of Architects New York Chapter

PROFESSIONAL AFFILIATIONS

Fellow, American Institute of Architects

William Van Alen

1882 Born in Brooklyn, New York

1898 Worked for Manhattan architect-developer Clarence True

ca. 1900 Studied at Pratt Institute, Brooklyn

1902 Worked as a draftsman for Clinton & Russell Architects

1908 Won a fellowship to study at l'École des Beaux-Arts, Paris

1911–25 Partnership with H. Craig Severance, Manhattan

1954 Died in New York

REPRESENTATIVE WORKS

1934 Prototype for a steel-clad, mass-producible house (now in Sea Gate, Brooklyn, New York)

1929 The Chrysler Building, New York City

1928 The Reynolds Building, New York City

1927 Lucky Strike storefront, New York City

Delman Shoe Store, New York City

1925 Childs Restaurant Building, New York City

1920 Bainbridge Building, New York City

Gidding Building, New York City

1915 Albemarle Building, New York City

1914 Standard Arcade, New York City

PROFESSIONAL AFFILIATIONS

Member of the American Institute of Architects

Fellow, National Academy of Design

Ludwig Mies van der Rohe

1886 Born in Aachen, Germany

1905–07 Worked for the architect and furniture designer Bruno Paul, Berlin

1908–11 Worked for Peter Behrens, Berlin

1912 Established a private practice in Berlin

1927 Directed the Weißenhofsiedlung, Stuttgart

1930 Appointed Director of the Bauhaus, Dessau

1932 Moved the Bauhaus from Dessau to Berlin (under pressure from the Nazis, the school was closed in 1933)

1938 Appointed the Director of the College of Architecture, Planning and Design at the Illinois Institute of Technology

1969 Died in Chicago, Illinois

SELECTED WORKS

1968 New National Gallery, Berlin

1967 The Martin Luther King Jr. Memorial Library, Washington, D. C.

1965 Social Service Administration Building, University of Chicago

1964 Federal Center (U.S. Courthouse and Federal Office and U.S. Post Office Building), Chicago, Illinois

1963 One Charles Center, Baltimore, Maryland

Home Federal Savings and Loan Association of Des Moines, Des Moines, Iowa

1961 Bacardi Building, Mexico City, Mexico

1959 Houston Museum of Fine Arts, Houston, Texas

1958 Seagram Building, New York

1956 Crown Hall (Architecture, City Planning and Design Building), Illinois Institute of Technology, Chicago, Illinois

1951 Lake Shore Drive Apartments, Chicago, Illinois

1950 Dr. Edith Farnsworth House, Plano, Illinois

1949 Promontory Apartments, Chicago, Illinois

1941 Illinois Institute of Technology campus, Chicago, Illinois

1930 Tugendhat House, Brno, Czech Republic

1929 German Pavilion for the Barcelona International Exposition, Barcelona, Spain (reconstructed in 1986)

1928 Hermann Lange House, Krefeld, Germany

1927 Weißenhof apartments, Stuttgart, Germany

1927 Municipal housing, Afrikanischestraße, Berlin

1926 Monument to Karl Liebknecht and Rosa Luxemburg, Berlin (destroyed by the Nazis; resurrected by the GDR)

1921 "Glass Skyscraper" (unbuilt)

1907 Riehl House, Neubabelsberg, Berlin

José Villagrán

1901 Born in Mexico City

1923 Graduated from the Escuela de Arquitectura de la Academia de San Carlos, Mexico City

1924–57 Professor at the School of Architecture (ENA), Universidad Nacional Autónoma de México (UNAM)

1933–35 Director of the ENA, UNAM

1935 Established a private practice in Mexico City

1951 Envoy to the World Health Organization, Washington, D. C.

1982 Died in Mexico City

SELECTED WORKS

1963 Tacubaya, La Viga and Coyoacán National Preparatory Schools of the UNAM, Mexico City

Bolivia Building, Mexico City

1961 Mier y Pesado Foundation Hospital, Mexico City

1958 Academy and Medical Congress Unit, National Medical Center, Mexico City

1958 Experimental Surgery and Resident Physicians Wards, National Institute of Cardiology, Mexico City

Santa Cruz Chapel, San Angel, Mexico

1957 Reforma Office Building and Movie Theater, Mexico City

1952 Mundet Maternity Clinic Access Ramp, Mexico City

1951 Escuela de Arquitectura y Museo de Arte, Ciudad Universitaria, Mexico City

1948 Parking Garage, Avenida Gante, Mexico City

1944 Mexico University Center, Mexico City

1943 Mundet Sports Park, Mexico City

Administrative buildings, Hospital de Jesús, Mexico City

1941 Children's Hospital, Mexico City

1937 National Institute of Cardiology, Mexico City

1934 Day School, Mexico City

1929 Child Hygiene Clinic, Mexico City

Milk Supplier, Popotla, Mexico

Tuberculosis Hospital, Huipulco

1925 Hygiene Institute, Popotla, Mexico

SELECTED AWARDS

1981 Premio Nacional de Arquitectura, Sociedad Mexicana de Ingenieros y Arquitectos

1968 Premio Nacional de Arte, Mêxico

PROFESSIONAL AFFILIATIONS

Member, El Colegio Nacional

Member, the Sociedad Mexicana de Arquitectos (President, 1926; Fellow, 1979)

Hans Busso von Busse

1930 Born in Opole, Silesia, Poland

1947–50 Apprenticeship in carpentry

1954 Graduated from the Technical University in Munich

1955 Master of Architecture, Massachusetts Institute of Technology

1956 Established a private practice in Munich

1971–75 President of the Bund Deutscher Architekten (BDA)

1981–84 Dean of the School of Architecture, Universität Dortmund

SELECTED WORKS

1996 Riem-Ost U-Bahn Station, Munich

Witten House (with Eberhard Klapp), Witten, Germany

1994 Bavarian Training Institute for the Handicapped, Munich

1992 Munich International Airport, Munich

1990 Grace Church, Würzburg, Germany

Municipal Archives, Munich

1988 IBA Project, Berlin

1983 Trade Center, Coburg, Germany

Dining Hall, Evangelical Lutheran Academy, Tutzing, Germany

1978 Urban rehabilitation, Coburg, Germany

1967 Church of the Holy Spirit, Schaftlach (burned in 1978)

1965 Indoor natatorium, Rheine, Germany

1964 Ithaca House, Hannoversch-Münden, Germany

1962 Erlöserkirche, Erding-Klettham, Germany

1959 Tegernsee House, Bavaria, Germany

SELECTED AWARDS

1993 Fritz Schumacher Prize for Architecture

1992 Prize for Architecture, awarded by the City of Munich

1965 Prize for the Advancement of Architecture, awarded by the City of Munich

1954 Otto Bartning Foundation Prize for Architecture

PROFESSIONAL AFFILIATIONS

Member, Bund Deutscher Architekten (BDA)

Member, Academy of Arts, Berlin

Member, Bavarian Academy of Fine Arts, Munich

Professor, Design and Building Construction, Universität Dortmund

Frank Lloyd Wright

1867 Born in Richland Center, Wisconsin

1886 Studied civil engineering at the University of Wisconsin, Madison

1888–93 Worked under Louis Sullivan at Adler and Sullivan, Chicago, Illinois

1893 Established a private practice in Chicago, Illinois

1905 First visit to Japan

1911 Publication of Wright's portfolio by Ernst Wasmuth, Berlin

1959 Died in Phoenix, Arizona

SELECTED WORKS

1959 Solomon R. Guggenheim Museum, New York

1959 Marin County Government Center, San Rafael, California

Greek Orthodox Church, Wauwatosa, Wisconsin

1957 Beth Shalom Synagogue, Elkins Park, Pennsylvania

1956 Harold Price Tower, Bartlesville, Oklahoma

1951 First Unitarian Church, Shorewood Hills, Wisconsin

1950 Johnson Wax Laboratory Tower, Racine, Wisconsin

V. C. Morris Gift Shop, San Francisco

1944 Jacobs ("Solar Hemicycle") House, Middleton, Wisconsin

1939 Johnson Wax Administration Building, Racine, Wisconsin

Fallingwater (Edgar J. Kaufmann House), Bear Run, Pennsylvania

1938 Taliesin West, Scottsdale, Arizona

1937 Hanna ("Honeycomb") House, Palo Alto, California

1936 Herbert Jacobs House, Madison, Wisconsin

1932 Taliesin Fellowship Complex, Spring Green, Wisconsin

1923 Millard House ("La Miniatura"), Pasadena, California

1922 Barnsdall House, Los Angeles, California

1921 Imperial Hotel, Tokyo (demolished 1968)

1914 Midway Gardens, Chicago, Illinois (demolished 1968)

1911–25 Taliesin East, Spring Green, Wisconsin

1910 Frederick C. Robie House, Chicago, Illinois

1909 City National Bank, Mason City, Iowa

1907 Unity Temple, Oak Park, Illinois

1905 Larkin Company Administration Building, Buffalo, New York (demolished 1950)

1904 Darwin D. Martin House, Buffalo, New York

1894 Winslow House, River Forest, Illinois

1889 Frank Lloyd Wright Home and Studio, Oak Park, Illinois

SUSAN GRAY is a portrait photographer and writer who has worked with a number of major corporations, magazines, and museums. The Eastman Kodak Company sponsored her first book, *Writers on Directors*. *Architects on Architects* was sponsored by the USG Corporation.

Pulitzer Prize–winning architecture critic PAUL GOLDBERGER is currently the architecture critic and a staff writer for *The New Yorker* and contributing writer to *Architectural Digest*. He is the author of several books, including *The City Observed: New York*, *The Skyscraper*, *On the Rise: Architecture and Design in a Post-Modern Age*, and *Above New York*. In addition to the Pulitzer, his writing has received numerous other awards, including the President's Medal of the Municipal Art Society of New York, the medal of the American Institute of Architects, and the Medal of Honor of the New York Landmarks Preservation Foundation.